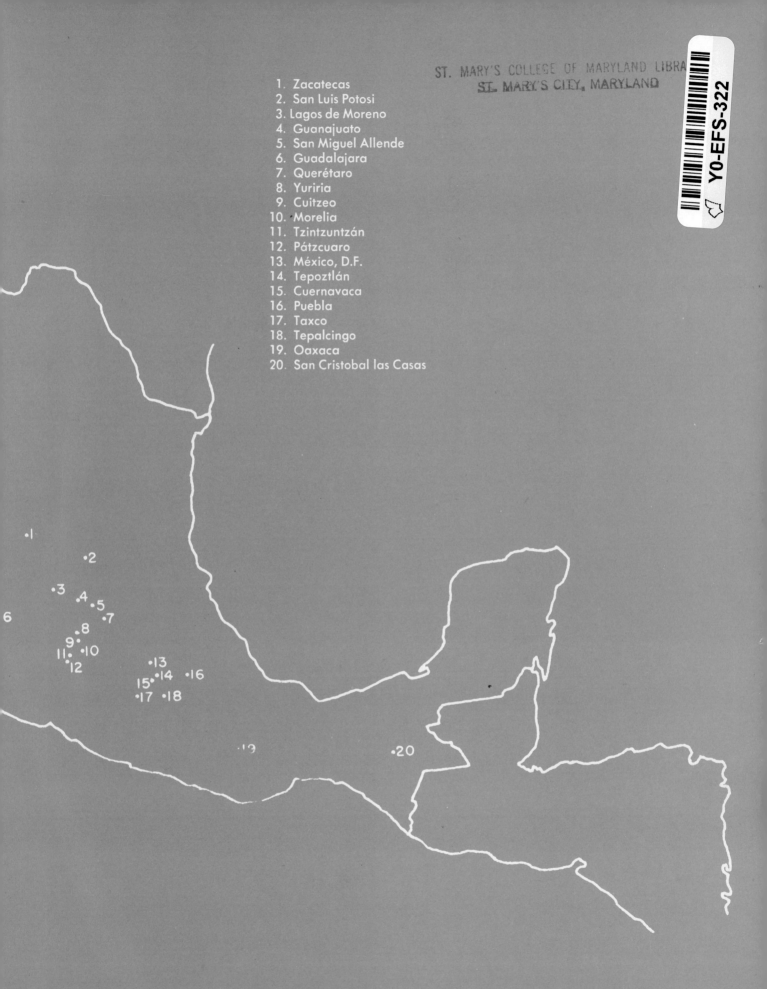

1. Zacatecas
2. San Luis Potosi
3. Lagos de Moreno
4. Guanajuato
5. San Miguel Allende
6. Guadalajara
7. Querétaro
8. Yuriria
9. Cuitzeo
10. Morelia
11. Tzintzuntzán
12. Pátzcuaro
13. México, D.F.
14. Tepoztlán
15. Cuernavaca
16. Puebla
17. Taxco
18. Tepalcingo
19. Oaxaca
20. San Cristobal las Casas

THE CHURCHES OF MEXICO

THE CHURCHES OF MEXICO
1530 ᨆ 1810

BY JOSEPH ARMSTRONG BAIRD, JR.

PHOTOGRAPHS BY

HUGO RUDINGER

UNIVERSITY OF CALIFORNIA PRESS

Berkeley and Los Angeles

1962

University of California Press
Berkeley and Los Angeles, California

Cambridge University Press
London, England

Designed by Rita Carroll

Printed in the United States of America

Plate 7 is reproduced with the kind permission of the
Instituto Nacional de Antropología e Historia, México

For
CHRISTL RUDINGER
and
DR. AND MRS. J. A. BAIRD, SR.

PREFACE

The serious literature, in English, on viceregal or colonial Mexican religious architecture and art is not large. Since Sylvester Baxter's pioneer study of 1901 (*Spanish-Colonial Architecture in Mexico*), there have been only a few works which have attempted and achieved accuracy of fact, integrity of scholarship, and sensitivity to the special character of the viceroyalty of New Spain. George Kubler's monumental study of the sixteenth century (*Mexican Architecture in the Sixteenth Century*); Elizabeth Wilder Weismann's perceptive survey of sculpture (*Mexico in Sculpture: 1521–1821*), which is often closely connected with architecture; the sections on Mexico in Pál Kelemen's wide-ranging study of Latin American seventeenth- and eighteenth-century developments (*Baroque and Rococo in Latin America*); and most recently George Kubler's and the late Martin Soria's notable contributions on the architecture and art of Spain and its colonies in the Pelican History of Art (*The Art and Architecture of Spain and Portugal and Their American Dominions: 1500–1800*)— these are the principal additions to knowledge of the subject in the English language. There have been a number of travel and historical books which have touched upon Mexican architecture and art, some vividly illuminating and others frankly journalistic. A few authors— architects rather than architectural historians—have provided readable though incomplete and partially inaccurate and dated studies of Mexican architecture (Sanford's *The Story of Architecture in*

Mexico). Most works in these latter categories have revealed little general acquaintance with art history; the result has been an inconsistent analysis of style, sources, and periods.

In other than the English language, there have been particularly valuable contributions in Spanish, as one would expect. To be especially noted are works by Angulo Íñiguez, Marco Dorta, and others in Spain. Angulo's contributions to Volumes I and II of *Historia del arte hispano-americano* contain one of the most thorough art historical surveys of the viceregal period in Mexico. In Mexico, the Instituto de Investigaciones Estéticas at the National University in Mexico City has been the principal fountainhead of scholarly studies—early under the Instituto's first director, Manuel Toussaint, and now under his successor, Justino Fernández. Toussaint's *Arte colonial* was but the summation of a distinguished career of writing on all aspects of viceregal art; Fernández' contributions to the two published catalogues of the provinces of Mexico, his study of later viceregal aesthetics and criticism in *Retablo de los Reyes,* the recent general survey in *Arte mexicano,* and numerous other works have added fresh interpretations and new material on the period. Of the investigators at the Instituto, Francisco de la Maza has especially devoted his attention to architecture from 1530 to 1810; other members of the staff, such as the late Flores Guerrero, and González Galván, Moyssén, Romero de Terreros, Vargas Lugo de Bosch, and Villegas, have continued to publish actively on various aspects of the era. Serious, scholarly studies by Europeans others than Spaniards have been rare. Gillet's section on Mexico in Michel's *Histoire de l'Art,* a few articles in German, and various picture books published recently (Kusch's *Mexiko im Bild*) have been general rather than specific.

The present work is not intended to be definitive nor all-inclusive. Examination of particular churches of Mexico from 1530 to 1810 will give the reader an insight into the major foci of architecture, sculpture, and the other arts in that period. Their principles can be applied to other monuments not specifically discussed in the text or Catalogue of Plates. The text has been written as a study of a complex subject which does not bypass any of the obvious problems of that subject but attempts to make those problems intelligible in terms of contemporary art historical scholarship. The Catalogue of Plates examines individual works more specifically. A Glossary offers definitions of historical and technical terms which may be new to the reader or need redefinition. Three Chronologies attempt to reduce historical sequences to schematic order, and Biographical Sketches of the leading architects expand the information given in the text. Drawings and maps also visually amplify objects and buildings in this study. A selective Bibliography provides critical reference to other studies.

Hugo Rudinger's photographs were taken with a 35-mm. Leica camera and were enlarged and printed by Mr. Rudinger. The exigencies of time and space made it impossible to include all photographs ideally indicated for such a book; preference was given to less commonly published buildings and to their most interesting features. Of the group selected, as wide a range as possible of period, building type, and special parts has been intended. The text and Catalogue of Plates can have full meaning only in terms of the values expressed in these selected photographs.

Acknowledgments

Among the acknowledgments that are due to the many individuals who have materially contributed to this book, particular recognition must go to Justino Fernández for his unfailing assistance at every stage of travel and research. Francisco de la Maza first kindled the author's enthusiasm for the churches of Mexico, and George Kubler has continued to provide an enviable model of scholarship as well as effective criticism. Margaret Collier generously shared her special study of Lorenzo Rodríguez and mid-eighteenth–century Mexico. Marion Dean Ross gave valuable suggestions for the Chronologies and Glossary, as did René C. Taylor, who also added important comments on the problems of architectural style. Robert Goebelt read and commented on the text. Joseph Thornhill was a receptive interpreter of figures and maps. Serge Millan checked parts of the Bibliography. For editorial assistance, a special debt of gratitude should be extended to Grace Wilson of the University of California Press, who saw the manuscript through its various stages of publication, and to August Frugé, Lucie E. N. Dobbie, and Mrs. Rita Carroll of the Press. Mrs. Patricia Garigliano showed unfailing competence and patience in transcribing and typing the manuscript; she was aided by Mrs. Alison Cramer, Mrs. Joyce MacFarlane, Raymond Rice, Clifford Ghames, and Celena Zeis. Finally, it is difficult to acknowledge adequately the general assistance of a large number of scholars and friends—especially Pál and Elisabeth Kelemen—who consistently encouraged the writing of this work. To them, to the members of the clergy, to all the generous people of contemporary Mexico, and to any others unwittingly neglected, the appreciation of author and photographer is expressed.

CONTENTS

List of Figures and Plates

Figures

PLATES

HUEJOTZINGO

CALPAN

TECAMACHALCO

TLALMANALCO

CUERNAVACA

SAN FRANCISCO ACATEPEC

TLACOCHAHUAYA

TEPOTZOTLÁN

TZINTZUNTZÁN

INTRODUCTION

The historical fact of the Spanish Conquest caused a distinct break in Mexican artistic history. The distinguished and varied expression of creative ability, in many art forms, of the Indian people who inhabited Mexico before A.D. 1521 was drastically altered in the destruction of the Aztec empire by the *conquistadores*. An Indian population outside Aztec dominion was eventually reduced to economic and religious vassalage, and thus were dissolved social and political patterns which had made the pre-Conquest arts possible. The degree of survival of pre-Conquest aesthetics and craftsmanship is still debated. An intense revival of nationalism in the nineteenth and twentieth century in Mexico brought forward champions of so-called Indian sources and of the mestizo and native-character theories in the arts. Not all were Mexican nationals; indeed, some of the most ardent proponents of these theories have been Europeans and North Americans.

Two important considerations are involved, especially in relation to architecture. The first is essentially aesthetic. In both the pre-Conquest Indian world and in pre-Renaissance [1] Spain, there was a tendency to unite architecture and ornamental sculpture in a particular way. Whether the actual character of the ornamental sculpture was geometric (as in the Mixtec area of Mexico and in Islamic art in Spain) or more naturalistic (as in the Aztec area of Mexico and in Gothic art

---

[1] Terms such as Renaissance, Mannerism, and Baroque are defined in the Glossary. Also, see Chronology I (p. 55) for a brief recapitulation of the eras of western European architecture and art.

in Spain), the result was a wedding of ornamental sculpture and architectural surfaces in a distinct decorative unity. A preference for strong contrasts of simple and complex in these ornamental surfaces was also marked.

In the post-Conquest era of Mexican architectural history, a new array of ornamental forms and sources became popular. In addition to the pre-Conquest and pre-Renaissance tendency to unite ornamental sculpture and architectural surfaces, a new tendency developed, modifying European sources to suit the skills of native craftsmen. This was essentially a technical matter. Local artisans adapted sixteenth-century Italian, Flemish, German, and Spanish forms to their abilities and preferences. At an early date designers and craftsmen simplified and reworked sources in a manner acceptable to local skill and judgment. Sometimes the modifications resulted in a stereotyping and desiccation of European sources, provincial in its pejorative sense —a connotation still clinging to the word "colonial." At other times, the creative imagination of local craftsmen developed variants that were colonial in a more inventive sense. Contemporaneously, and more important for this book, sophisticated uses of these same sources and technical forms were marked in town and country. The inimitable personal brilliance of Mexican designers and craftsmen was consistently evolving in metropolitan and regional patterns.

The intermingling of these two tendencies—one aesthetic and the other technical—has caused much of the confusion about so-called Indian sources and native character. It seems clear that direct survivals of pre-Conquest artistic forms were short-lived after 1530. Application of pre-Conquest symbolism to the post-Conquest arts was comparatively limited. In sculpture (notably in the atrium crosses of the monasteries) and in painting, there were definite reminiscences of pre-Conquest forms and style. It would be absurd, too, to deny the importance to the friar-builders of a well-established pre-Conquest native technical mastery of stonecutting, carving, and stuccoing. Still, obvious direct survivals had almost disappeared by 1570 or 1580.

Throughout the entire viceregal period the two tendencies mentioned earlier continued to be manifest. Sometimes the first reinforced the second, as when the geometric proclivities of the Islamic world reinforced the technical stereotyping of curvilinear Renaissance and post-Renaissance motifs into flattened patterns. What one might call a sense of organized pattern in viceregal ornamental sculpture, especially as related to architecture, showed Mexico's continuing enthusiasm for over-all surface design in place of an interest in individual motifs or individual figure sculpture. Sometimes, unsophisticated craftsmanship (effective as it might be on nontechnical levels), produced works that were simply local rather than Indian. Yet, if one carefully studies the forms used in metropolis or province after 1530, or relates figure sculpture and painting to sources, one consistently finds a non-Indian European background.

It will never be feasible to separate entirely these aesthetic and technical considerations from the total artistic character of the viceregal era. Whether metropolitan or local, the result was inevitably imbued with a special Mexican flavor. Furthermore, it is impossible to assume that "metropolitan" was equal to "sophisticated" and that "local" was equal to "naïve" or "provincial." Some of the most fascinating works were in the provinces and showed a remarkable degree of ornamental and technical sophistication in regional styles; some of the dullest variants of European sources were in the capital. More than national economic and political factors were involved. The facts of specific area, patronage, the amount of funds, and the directing artistic personalities established a more logical hierarchy of values. It is perhaps as important for a modern viewer to respond to the special existing qualities of the arts as to be unduly concerned about sources. Still, one must guard against too easy acceptance of aesthetic and technical misconceptions, and particularly against the bland assumption that everything less sophisticated is necessarily more "Indian."

In addition to the overemphasized problem of the Indian background, one faces the more immediate problem of the European and particularly the Hispanic background of viceregal Mexican architecture and art. From beginning to end, the viceregal period was filled with successive waves of influence from the Old World to the New. Curiously enough, despite the attempts of certain writers to prove the contrary, virtually no important instances of artistic influence from Mexico to Spain can be documented. From the time of the earliest friar-builders to Manuel Tolsá's Neo-Classical voyage of artistic conquest at the end of the eighteenth century, there was a constant stream of itinerant designer-architects, master craftsmen, painters, and sculptors from various parts of Europe, seeking preferment and success

in the viceroyalty of New Spain. It is important to recognize the nature
and extent of the generally sequential change of fashion and style. It
came especially from northern Europe, with its close political ties to
Spain, and from southern Spain, with its close economic and administrative ties to New Spain. This changing pattern was imposed upon
Mexican architecture in the immemorial manner of any conquest.

The waves of influence from the Old World would seem to deny to
Mexico any power of initiation or any degree of originality in the for-
mation of its artistic character in the viceregal era. This, happily, was
not the case. From the beginning of the new age of Catholic Christianity to the end of the viceroyalty, there were not only highly original
combinations of Old World sources, but new combinations and effects
that had few direct parallels in the Old World. As a result, an artistic
history of remarkable unevenness and richness evolved. Between
Spain and Mexico a rather obvious parallel can be drawn with ancient
Rome and the Near East. In each case there were achievements in the
"dependent" that paralleled and in many ways went beyond the implications of the "parent," and at the same time simplifications in the
"dependent" that responded to wholly different aesthetic conventions
than those imposed by the "parent." The increased complexities of
this relationship between Spain and Mexico are apparent in the fact
that Spain was herself both "dependent" (on Rome, the Islamic
world, the Gothic North, and so on) and "parent."

This explanation should aid in removing some of the unfortunate
connotations of the word "colonial," which are often applied to viceregal Mexico. That it was a "dependent" politically is entirely true,
and yet Mexico's artistic development from 1530 to 1810 was anything
but a servile imitation of a master type created for export to the
colonies. The dynamics of both human and aesthetic destiny made that
impossible. Within the colonial status of Mexico there began that irre-
sistible development of national consciousness which has ultimately
modified all imperial and royal dominions, both artistically and politically. The creation of a class of mixed ethnic background—the
mestizo of the New World—inevitably modified the personal and artistic training and taste imposed by the foreign-born administrators
and itinerants of later generations. The psychology of ethnic mixture is
too complex for discussion here; furthermore, it has often been subject
to emotional rather than scientific interpretation. Let it suffice to say

that the mestizo inevitably responded to a different range of aesthetic stimuli than did the Spanish-born or the *criollo* (a person of Spanish parentage, born in the New World). But even these latter two were faced with a breadth of experience diverging from the traditions of Spain. The interaction of human and artistic forces created a milieu of intense vigor and interchange.

Within Mexico, certain factors militated against any complete metropolitan dominance (and by that is meant essentially Mexico City) of the brilliant architectural and artistic developments in the provinces. By the eighteenth century, every significant community in Mexico had become the focus of a distinctive local character in architecture and art, resulting in the considerable and easily seen difference of, say, Oaxaca and Guanajuato, or of Morelia and Puebla. It was these local schools which accounted for the special regional flavor of most later viceregal architecture and art. George Kubler [2] has suggested a "northern" and "southern" division of art from 1650 onwards in Mexico. Though his examples are well chosen, there are a number of exceptions to such a distinction—which Kubler bases on an "academic northern" (Mexico City and the north) and a "progressive southern" (Puebla and Oaxaca) trend. Much of "southern" design was as conservative as that of the "north" (which tended to be more "progressive" after 1750 because of the great new mineral discoveries and large-scale agricultural developments). Furthermore, the basically random scattering of formal relationship, based on the movement of architect, designers, and craftsmen from Mexico City both north and south, makes a consistent north-south contrast difficult.

The presence of certain geological materials was an important determining factor in the regional variety of Mexican viceregal architecture and its adornment, especially after 1680. The reddish pumice (*tezontle*) and gray-white limestone (*chiluca*) of Mexico City, the green-brown stone of Oaxaca, the variations from green to ashes of roses and brown in the stone of the Guanajuato–San Miguel area, the pink trachyte of Morelia, as well as the man-made tile of Puebla—all conferred a particular local character on metropolis and province. Within the limitations of these materials (tile tended to be more nationally diffused in the eighteenth century, especially on church

[2] *Art and Architecture in Spain and Portugal and Their American Dominions: 1500–1800*, pp. 76–78.

domes), local designer-builders interpreted the complex combinations of international, metropolitan, and regional forces that entered into any individual building. It is significant that one of the most powerful figures in Mexican architecture in the eighteenth century, Lorenzo Rodríguez, although born in Spain and apparently partly trained there, became an ardent proponent of local materials and evolved a style out of Spanish forms and his Mexican experience to suit those materials. Had the famous Sagrario by Rodríguez for Mexico City Cathedral been executed in imported white marble (as was such an eclectic modern building as the Opera-Palace of Fine Arts), it would never have had such a pronounced influence on the Mexican architecture of its time nor revealed such individual artistic quality.

It is interesting that the capital generally resisted that complete absorption of local taste which created a Oaxaca style, a Pueblan style, or a Querétaro style. As the center of political, economic, and religious power (even though that power was delegated from the mother country), Mexico City had a unique role in the colonial era. Its potentialities for patronage and its quick response to successive waves of fashion made Mexico City the unofficial center of architecture—the standard of fashion, the measure of social primacy. Though its buildings were thus set apart in variety and sometimes in number from others in the viceroyalty, many of the capital's finest projects were still conditioned by the materials at hand. This gave to the older parts of the city a special flavor, apparent today.

In Mexico City itinerant European architect-designers and craftsmen received favor throughout the viceregal era, although local masters often commanded important commissions in all the arts, especially in the eighteenth century. There was no central academy of the arts, no special school of architecture, to set an official seal of approval on one building form or another; that came only with the more pedantic developments of the Neo-Classical era. Here was a distinct factor for good, eliminating the aesthetic tyranny of an academy. Also, until well into the eighteenth century, comparatively few architectural "circles" or schools developed around individual masters in capital or province. There were, to be sure, regional variations of some cleric's or designer's fashionable innovations, as well as local schools of stuccoists or ornamentalists; before 1730, however, it would be difficult to conceive of Mexican art as essentially similar to Italian art with its numerous schools of the great masters. As a result, though itinerant designers from Europe brought to the viceroyalty new fashions which ultimately spread from capital to province, there was altogether a more elastic situation in terms of creative allegiance than might have been expected in a colonial area.

The matter of architectural training and status in capital or regional area is difficult to explain in a few sentences. Some architects were trained as carpenters rather than designers; some were essentially sculptors turned ornamental architectural designers. A fairly rigid and often intrigue-ridden code of acceptance by one's peers, on the basis of actual building, was generally used to determine competence. In the patronage system of the period many occasions for bias arose, and the archives are full of suits and complaints on this score.

A major aspect of later viceregal Mexican religious building remains to be mentioned in this Introduction. This was a general indifference to the full implications of Baroque planning, as used in certain parts of Europe after the middle of the seventeenth century. It is not that the word Baroque has no meaning for the churches of Mexico, but rather that a complex planning of interior and exterior, with particular attention to over-all integration of mass, surface, and space, was rare in Mexico. By its concentration on certain parts of a building complex (notably the fronts of churches and the great altar screens inside), Mexico forced its genius into a special flowering. The preoccupation with walls rather than spaces, with ornamental surfaces rather than the manipulation of mass, was an old tradition in both Mexico and Spain. It was this emphasis on certain salient parts of a building which gave Hispanic and especially Mexican architecture after 1530 some of its remarkable character.

The fascination with a complex integration of interior and exterior space which developed particularly during the later seventeenth and eighteenth century in Italy, France, England, and Germany had Classical antecedents. It went back to the Forum of Trajan, the Villa of Hadrian, and the remarkable late Roman planning in the Near East. The Early Christian world emphasized a simpler plan of sequential rather than interlocking spaces. Units of rectangular or rectilinear form, related by porches, forecourts, and stairways, followed an orderly progress from entrance to sacred area at the back. This plan was ultimately related to the Egyptian temple and to later Roman variants of that plan. The main unit of an Early Christian complex was invariably a high box with clerestory lighting. In the medieval, especially the Gothic, period in the West, the relation of church and town setting was frequently casual, despite instances of the planning of towns and fortifications. Unless a natural eminence enhanced the silhouette of a building, as at Chartres in France, one often came upon a medieval church of continental Europe by surprise.

Renaissance Italy tended to a more mathematically sophisticated combination of interior and exterior, as in Bramante's design for the new church of St. Peter in Rome. The later sixteenth century devoted itself to oppressive or unresolved spatial and structural effects, laying the foundations for a remarkable inventiveness in planning. By the seventeenth century, Italian architects had evolved a special competence in handling complex interior spaces, curvilinear exteriors, and the relation of both through light, rich materials, and ornamental sculpture. Gradually—and admittedly the effort was sporadic and often incomplete—these complex structures and interior spaces were related to their settings by the use of open spaces and colonnades, of richly modulated form carefully conceived in terms of scale. Throughout Europe, in varying degrees of bravura and scale and at various removes in time, the implications of Roman Baroque planning and structural innovations became increasingly important. There was no set pattern or consistency of means and ends, but there was a vital concern with over-all planning as a concept of design. Thus Versailles consisted of related spaces in one section of the palace (the Hall of Mirrors area), with a rabbit warren of rooms strung out in wings beyond. Yet the relation of the central and subordinate blocks of buildings to the axis of the garden was carefully contrived and ingenious in its utilization of old and new elements.

Spain had an ambiguous heritage of architectural planning. The Islamic designers had set the stage for carefully controlled relationships of spaces and structure, although the spaces themselves were generally simple repetitions of units rather than interpenetrating hollows. Visigothic, Romanesque, and Gothic construction had laid virtually no emphasis on total planning, although a kind of hierarchy of parts was obtained by the simple process of adding new sections to older structures. It is significant that the great medieval church of Santiago at Compostela waited until the eighteenth century for a monumental façade which would properly preface this revision of a revision. Examples of Renaissance and Mannerist structures and space appeared in the sixteenth century in Spain. Spain never whole-heartedly embraced the Baroque, and it was generally only under French and Italian influence in the eighteenth century that approximations of Late Baroque scale and relations of spaces were possible (La Granja of San Ildefonso and the new Royal Palace in Madrid). The Church of San Ignacio at Loyola was one of the few examples of Italian Baroque design principles applied to late seventeenth-century Spanish architecture.

If interest in and use of the full implications of Late Baroque planning were sporadic and inconsistent in Spain, they were even less common in Mexico. The sixteenth-century Mexican monastic complexes had been based on Early Christian planning traditions, with large forecourts or atriums, sometimes preceded by flights of stairs, and with a high boxlike church at the back of the court. In the medieval manner of western Europe, porches and patios were used to provide entrance and the necessary light and air for the monastic quarters.

The grid-form town plan of early viceregal Mexico, based on ancient Roman and especially on progressive, idealizing Renaissance planning —which was, in fact, less developed in Europe than in the New World —paralleled some aspects of pre-Christian Indian town planning of the Aztec period. The grid had open spaces at the intersection of main avenues, for church, market, and so on; this town site organization by the friars was not unlike the fairly regular pattern of certain tribal centers around ancient Mexico City (Tenochtitlán). In general, most pre-Conquest Indian ceremonial sites were not urban tribal centers like Aztec Tenochtitlán. They were sacred ensembles of buildings related through variations of height and stepped terraces with open spaces between. Ironically, the kind of urban planning which the friars organized carried out more consistently the urban ideas of the recently destroyed Aztec empire. Alone among the pre-Conquest Indian groups the Aztecs and their contemporaries in the Valley of Mexico had developed a distinctive town life that was something more than groups of houses near ceremonial areas, as it has been with the Maya and others.

Very soon after the Conquest, major structures were placed at salient points of the grid-planned towns, with large open spaces before or around them—some enclosed, others not. However, designers in Mexico, as in much of Europe, were generally indifferent to the careful integration of such structures and spaces. Despite their use of the grid and the truly remarkable majesty of town plans and plazas, it was not until well into the eighteenth century that arcades (*portales*) were importantly employed to surround plazas and relate peripheral buildings to them. Although its history has not yet been firmly plotted, the planning of the Zócalo (the main open space or plaza) and the Cathedral of Mexico is revealing. The "old" cathedral was within this Zócalo. The "new" (present) cathedral was at the north edge of the great plaza. Yet the landscaping of the area between Cathedral and Zócalo—resulting in the nineteenth century in an effective, if irregular, arrangement of rows of trees fronting on a public square and parade ground—never became *consistently* involved in the over-all plan concepts of the Late Baroque. The arrangement of parts at the great shrine of Guadalupe (essentially of the eighteenth century and later) was equally interesting. Before the recent paving of the area around the Basilica, there was little actual integration of the shrine proper with the two functional elements of the complex—the place of the vision of the Madonna on the Hill of Tepeyac, and the miraculous well below. Their only connection was in rambling stairs and courtyards; the few ideal plans and projects on paper for major buildings (such as the Cathedral of Mexico or the Basilica of Guadalupe) were generally unrealized in viceregal times.

Though Mexico developed numerous pilgrimage churches in later viceregal times, she showed less enthusiasm than did Portugal and Brazil for the elaborate type of Late Baroque pilgrimage church with carefully planned stairways and dependencies. Nevertheless, a few examples of pilgrimage churches of this kind were built in Mexico—at Tlacotepec (the Santuario de Nuestro Señor del Calvario) in a firm way, and at San Pablo Ostotepec in a timid way. Pilgrimage churches with stairs of access in more casual patterns were built at Amecameca and at Cholula (Nuestra Señora de los Remedios).

The intention of the first friar-builders had been to create practical ensembles of Spanish Catholic culture in an alien setting; their monastic complexes succeeded admirably in doing so. The later viceroys and the nobility were, for various reasons, reluctant to cope with immense planning schemes, though certain of them (Bucareli, for example) initiated important street revisions and civic improvements. In general, the town plans of the friars were taken over and embellished with individual monuments of personal aggrandizement, luxury, or piety. The patronage system made it mandatory for ambitious architects and builders to attach themselves to a high cleric, a noble, a person of wealth, or one of the religious or civic groups which sponsored building. The inevitable result was a series of structures, civic or ecclesiastic, that were tributes to the patron or the organization. Add to this the constant atmosphere of suspicion and intrigue which enveloped Spain and Mexico between 1530 and 1810. Undue "pretension" on the part of any individual or group was suspect. The architects themselves were engaged in constant bickering and energy-consuming lawsuits which reduced opportunities to carry major projects to completion under orderly circumstances. It is all the more remarkable that so much construction was achieved. The number of churches built or revised in the viceregal period has never been accurately counted. Estimates running into the thousands have been suggested, but it would take a corps of more than human cataloguers to complete the task of searching out each country church, hacienda chapel,[3] and shrine, to say nothing of the relatively well-documented town and city monuments.

It would be foolish to pretend to definitiveness in so brief a summary of the indifference of Mexican designers to consistent use of an over-all complexity of structure and plan found in certain parts of Late Baroque Europe. From the time of the sixteenth-century monasteries and hospitals to the great eighteenth-century *colegios*, a fine sense of space and plan invested certain parts of Mexican religious buildings. Stair halls in Mexico, as in Spain, were often of magnificent architectural character. Interior patios had an amplitude and order which only gradually developed in the related arcades of exterior plazas. The open chapel of the sixteenth century, the Rosary chapel of the seventeenth century, the *camarín* of the eighteenth century were brilliant adventures in the use of space and ornament. The church itself, however, rarely strayed from Early Christian concepts of interior plan and elevation or from medieval or Renaissance variants of the

[3] It is socially significant that Mexico was a country of haciendas rather than villas. The agricultural imperialism of the hacienda mirrored the political imperialism of the Spanish system.

basilica.[4] After 1630, the use of the Gesù-inspired [5] deep apse and transept as chapels was common in non-cathedral churches. Century in and century out, however, variations on the box with clerestory remained popular. Related structures were adjacent to, not part of, the smaller church's fabric. (The physical size of cathedral churches made inclusion of certain features inevitable; but the Sagrario was distinctly isolated from the fabric of the Cathedral of Mexico.)

Within the church, decorative features were sometimes treated with little apparent regard for a total visual or psychological unity. Styles were freely mixed, especially in the eighteenth century. Still, one must guard against a too easy criticism of architectural "impurity." A consistent high level of taste and craftsmanship helped to link periods, which often had underlying connections in common sources of inspiration, no matter how modified in later developments. Furthermore, a preoccupation with the concept of grandeur (*la grandeza mexicana*) as a leading principle of design and religious life gave seventeenth- and eighteenth-century Mexico a special association with the wellsprings of the Baroque ethos.

Thus, though there was no consuming or consistent interest in overall planning of intricately conceived mass, curvilinear space, and interlocking structural parts, there was much of the impetus of the Baroque in colonial Mexico's later architectural history. It took the form of the development of ornamental façades and altar screens, and of special chapels and *camarines*, with richly plastic parts and dramatic lighting. A color glamour of tile, of curiously mixed technical and decorative origins, was cast over lofty staged domes in a typically Baroque crescendo of accents. Furthermore, it would be impossible to isolate properly the peculiar Mexican *genius loci*, so well seen at Taxco or at San Cayetano de La Valenciana above Guanajuato. Neither Santa Prisca at Taxco or San Cayetano had the structural ingenuity of a Vierzehnheiligen,[6] and yet both were distinctly Baroque in their towering silhouettes and climaxes of effect in dazzling façades and interior retables. It would be as impossible to define the innate sensibility of Mexican designers to the continuity and contrasts of material and color as it would be to define the equally inspired sensitivity of the

---

[4] Santa Brígida in Mexico City was a rare exception.

[5] The Italian architect Vignola's church for the Jesuit order in Rome was especially influential in Catholic countries.

[6] Neumann's eighteenth-century pilgrimage church near Lichtenfels, Germany.

great masters of Europe. One can but point out certain qualities and attempt to place them in a coherent framework. Each traveler and student can add his own aura to them in Mexico.

With these introductory concepts and considerations, it will be easier to make a more thorough study of building types and the sequence of fashions and styles in the adornment of those building types in Mexico from 1530 to 1810, as well as to review something of the Spanish background. For convenience and clarity I have divided viceregal Mexican art history into roughly fifty-year eras. This arrangement, as close to consistency of scheme as possible, helps to relate the various centuries and their major developmental phases. (See Chronologies II and III [pp. 56–57] for the relation of these divisions in Spain and Mexico.) The three great building periods in Mexico were from about 1530 to 1580, from 1630 to 1680, and especially from 1730 to 1780. Most of the churches of the viceroyalty of New Spain were initiated or substantially completed in these periods. However, the person who wishes to find pleasure in a study of the churches of Mexico should never let too rigorous systematization destroy for him the extraordinary qualities of the individual monument and the local place.

I

The Spanish Background

Few eras in the history of architecture have been so misrepresented in popular writing as the viceregal period of Mexico.[1] Errors of fact and judgment, slowly and carefully eliminated from critical scholarship over many years, have continued to be repeated to the layman. The ageless exaggerations of popular myth and romantic history invest buildings, giving false impressions of the remote and immediate past. Part of this falseness is based on a limited understanding of fundamental changes in architectural and art history since A.D. 1500, especially in relation to Spain. The increasing importance of the role of

---

[1] The word "viceregal" historically delimits the period when Mexico was the viceroyalty of New Spain. This era is often called the "colonial" period, although, when applied to aesthetics, that designation can be extended beyond the end of the viceroyalty. Furthermore, "colonial" has political and economic overtones unpleasant to modern Mexico. Nuances of meaning may suggest the use of "viceregal" or "colonial" in certain contexts in this study. For the present work on the churches of Mexico in this brilliantly creative period it seemed wiser to provide the beginning and end dates of 1530 and 1810 as preferable to either "viceregal" or "colonial" or the usual dates of 1521 and 1821. Serious construction did not begin until a few years *after* the conquest of Aztec Mexico City in 1521. 1530 is a reasonable compromise date and relates more effectively to the Chronologies used here. The great changes in viceregal religious architecture were about over by 1790 or 1800, when the Neo-Classical became dominant. 1810, however, is both historically an end of the old order, with Father Hidalgo's Independence movement, and includes the last flourishes of the architectural *grandeza* of that order.

Mannerism in both Europe and the New World; the character and regional variations of Baroque—or indeed the very existence of such a concept, long accepted by scholars; the special relationship of Spain and Mexico in the seventeenth and eighteenth centuries; all the problems discussed in the Introduction—these are often cast aside in favor of interpretations by certain early writers on Mexico who were unaware of its special qualities and incapable of reading more nicely the equation of Spain and the viceroyalty.

The technical language of architecture and art has been at best only half understood by these writers, and the lack of any fixed descriptive language for the changes of style or fashion has caused endless confusion. Since this book is a study of viceregal Mexican churches, a brief recapitulation of Spanish architectural history relevant to Mexico is needed.[2] The European background of painting and sculpture in Mexico between 1530 and 1810 (much of which appears in the decoration of churches) is, in part, discussed later in chapter iii. Kubler and Soria provide a more complete survey in their work for the Pelican History of Art (*The Art and Architecture of Spain and Portugal and Their American Dominions: 1500–1800*). Additional references can be found in the Bibliography of the present book.

Spanish architecture and art were something other than local European styles. More than any of the great European nations, Spain revealed a breadth and complexity of source and regional variation in its architecture and art that would be almost impossible to survey adequately. The pre-Roman period is essentially unrelated to the present study, although vestigial survivals of this era continued into later epochs. Roman engineering and technical resources were gradually modified by interaction with Barbarian (largely Visigothic) influences and later by the addition of vigorous new stocks of Romanesque French and German-French Gothic—all of this primarily in the northern and eastern parts of Spain. In the south the important aesthetic and material conventions of Islamic architecture and art appeared from about A.D. 800 on. There were inevitable interrelations of the southern and northeastern, especially on the borders of each sphere of influence (for example, in Toledo). Thus up to A.D. 1500 the south had a distinct Roman-Islamic character, and the northeast a more Romanesque-Gothic one.

[2] For an outline of the architectural history of Spain, see Chronology II (p. 56).

The reduction of the Moors' territory, especially after A.D. 1500, prepared the south for new artistic forces. The waning of late medieval monasticism and the rise of town government in the north relaxed the hold of the Gothic, although medieval traditions died slowly. The primary influence of the post-Islamic and medieval era was, of course, the revival of Classical antiquity in the Italian Renaissance—in itself a constant revision of Classical traditions by brilliant new interpreters of form, space, and ornament. This first, fairly "pure," phase of Renaissance architecture, essentially that of Tuscany, Italy, had comparatively limited importance in Spain, except for ornament (figs. 25, 26, and 28). Many of the architects of sixteenth-century Spain referred to their work as *a lo romano;* however, though there was a phase of interest in a variant of purist Italian Renaissance-Mannerist design late in the sixteenth century (the Herreran style), most of sixteenth-century Spanish work was a combination of Gothic, Islamic, and Renaissance in varying proportions. Discussion of the Spanish mixing of fashions in the sixteenth century during the so-called Plateresque period will be found in chapter iii.

Of particular importance after A.D. 1550, partly because of the peculiar international political character of Spain in this period, was Mannerism. Mannerism had two main variants—that of Italy and that of northern Europe (particularly Flanders and Germany). The Habsburg rulers of Spain and the Low Countries united in their domains proponents of both variants, and thus both came to Mexico in the sixteenth century. Imperfect understanding of the role of Mannerism and its special character in Spain has led to an imperfect appreciation of much Spanish and Mexican architecture and art after 1550. As much as the celebrated Moorish (Islamic) influence of Spain on Mexico, Mannerism influenced a special part of post-Renaissance Hispanic architecture and art. This does not mean that one should overemphasize its role, but simply give it proper due.

Following the period of Renaissance and Mannerist influence, there began that most vivid era, the Baroque.[3] The Baroque was unquestionably a major creative impulse of the period from 1580 to 1780, with the special exceptions noted in the Introduction. As in preceding eras,

---

[3] A convenient and effective modern analysis of both Mannerism and Baroque can be found in Nikolaus Pevsner's *Outline of European Architecture*, which unfortunately presents certain misconceptions in the relations of later Baroque Spain and Mexico.

there was a considerable involvement with the tastes of the past. The final product was enriched by many sources; in southern Spain Islamic remembrances were still important, but the character of most individual works was Baroque. Mannerism had a persisting influence and continued to affect much of the later Baroque of both south and north.

The troublesome term Churrigueresque [4] appears in reference to a part of this period. This word has had particular currency in Mexico, but not in the sense that Mexican work is directly related to the Churriguera family of architects (especially José de Churriguera the Younger). In Spain, the Churriguera family had a major part in developing the architectural styles of both Madrid and Salamanca during the seventeenth and eighteenth centuries. The Churrigueras' interests were essentially Baroque, although strongly mixed with Renaissance and Mannerist survivals. However, they had no role to play in Sevilla or Granada, the two principal centers of influence for Mexico.

The word Churrigueresque can mean something in Mexico only if one creates a new connotation with the term Mexican Churrigueresque. This term, not accurate nor historically appropriate but sanctioned by usage, which may partially describe those eighteenth-century Mexican architectural and artistic developments, is now especially connected with the name of Lorenzo Rodríguez. Rodríguez was a Spaniard from Guadix who played a dominant role in determining Mexico's architectural development from 1730 to 1780—a period when an important part of viceregal church architecture was constructed or revised. Some writers have favored Ultra-Baroque as a more satisfactory term than Mexican Churrigueresque, but neither is really adequate. Ultra-Baroque implies something consistently *beyond* the implications of Baroque in Europe, in both conception and execution. This is historically unfair to the special character of much eighteenth-century Mexican architecture and ornamental sculpture. The refinements and problems of these terms will be explored more fully in chapter iii.

Spanish architecture and art of the later seventeenth and eighteenth century contained most of the immediate inspiration for changes of style and fashion in Mexico. It was the south of Spain (Andalucía especially) which produced most of the men and forms that determined

---

[4] Lorente Junquera's article in the *Encyclopedia of World Art* offers a contemporary study in English of Churrigueresque, or what some scholars prefer to call Churrigueran.

Map of Spain.

these changes in Mexico. There were interesting parallel developments in other parts of Spain which were echoed in Mexico, but it was from Granada-Córdoba and Sevilla and the towns along the roads to Cádiz that the principal impulses for the many mutations of ornament and design in Mexico emanated. Recent research has turned attention to the role of both Francisco Hurtado and his circle in Granada-Córdoba, and to Gerónimo Balbás from Sevilla-Cádiz. Both men were Late Baroque in their fundamental approach to design, but Balbás added a strong interest in Mannerist forms.

Hurtado's work is still being studied, and disputes continue over the exact nature of his contributions to works particularly relevant to Mexico. Although he never left Spain, he unquestionably played a major role in Mexican architecture of the eighteenth century, essentially through the influence of his work on other designer-architects and on those who went to Mexico. The future will discover a widening circle of contact between this brilliant figure and his associates and the relations of areas within southern Spain, and of those same areas with Mexico. Balbás, who traveled from Sevilla to Cádiz and the New World, was ably "succeeded" in Mexico by Lorenzo Rodríguez, creator of a special fusion of forms related to those of both Hurtado and Balbás.

Besides the strong infusion of Baroque scale, focus, and light effects into eighteenth-century Spain and the various regional centers of style, two new flavors were added to the already heady artistic mixture of that era. These were the Rococo and the Neo-Classical. Rococo, connected in its origins with the French background and culture of the royal house of Spain at this period, came to southern Spain about 1755 or 1760, and was especially developed after 1770. It had a greater vogue in Sevilla, Jerez, and Cádiz than in Granada-Córdoba, but as in most of Europe it was confined to interior rather than exterior architecture. Essentially a decorative and furniture style, it had most influence on plaster work and wooden carvings, especially in *rocaille,* or rock and shell patterns (fig. 36).

The interest in Neo-Classical forms was evident in southern Spain throughout the eighteenth century. Before 1770 this interest was expressed as a form of *classicizing* Baroque. After 1770 and 1780 there was a move to revive purer ancient Greek and Roman forms. The Neo-Classical as such played a less important role in southern Spain than in Mexico, where it was of great influence. When one sees Andalusian towns, there is never an immediate impression of temple fronts and colonnades such as appear in Celaya, Mexico. Indeed, much of the great Andalusian architecture and art of earlier periods was spared the fashion-motivated destruction, especially of church interiors, that occurred in Mexico about 1800.

It is difficult to generalize about Spanish, and especially Andalusian, architecture toward the end of the eighteenth century. Madrid's attempted imposition of academic Neo-Classical taste on the regional areas was erratic and uncoördinated. Spain continued to exercise its Rococo– and Neo-Classical–oriented tastes in terms of Baroque scale and often with essentially Baroque light effects, despite the growth of monochromatic Neo-Classical interior color enthusiasms. There was no single regional architect in Andalucía, like Francisco Eduardo Tresguerras in Mexico, who wholeheartedly reworked an entire area in Neo-Classical variants of the Late Baroque.

II

The Churches of Mexico
BUILDING TYPES

By a curious historical coincidence, the three periods of Mexican vice-regal architecture and art which especially mirror the changing relation of religion to building occupy the same general space of time in three sequential centuries. Thus the eras from about 1530 to 1580, from about 1630 to 1680, and from about 1730 to 1780 each reflect the special character of three major developmental phases of art in Mexico from the Conquest to the break with Spain.[1] It would be unwise to minimize the roles of the eras between. However, by concentrating here on the three periods listed, one can obtain a more concise and at the same time more penetrating insight into the particular qualities of viceregal Mexican architecture and art. A general survey of the essence of this sequence will permit a vivid resumé of forms and artistic interests in different eras. The generalizations and caveats of the Introduction and of the previous chapter on Spain will then serve as a means of interpreting their nuances.

A simple distinction of the three great periods in terms of religious building form can be made as follows: The period from 1530 to 1580 was the age of the monastery. The period from 1630 to 1680 was the age of the initiation or effective structural completion of the great

---

[1] Certain figures (pp. 46–53) will clarify parts of this chapter; see also end paper map.

metropolitan cathedrals. The period from 1730 to 1780 was the age of climax for magnificent new or redecorated parish and pilgrimage churches. It might seem that this outline is too neat and therefore presents a false interpretation of facts. In its main elements, however, it is a useful guide, though one must guard against too rigid schematization.

Monastic Churches

From the peculiarly important role of the monastic clergy's missionary activity among the newly conquered Indians, previously under Aztec rulers, it was obvious that a proliferation of the spheres of influence of the various brotherhoods would result in proliferation of their monastic houses. There was a somewhat differing intellectual and spiritual tone to the three monastic orders active in Mexico in the sixteenth century—the Franciscans, the Dominicans, and the Augustinians. This, as well as the differing emphases placed upon the formal interrelation of art and religion, inevitably produced monastic complexes of a distinctly individual character for the Franciscans, largely in the central but also in the western part of Mexico, the Dominicans south of Mexico City to Oaxaca, and the Augustinians in the northwestern and western areas overlapping with the Franciscan regions.

All three orders were faced with the same general problem—that of building a basic group of architectural units (such as church, monastery, and service elements), using local craftsmen and labor under the supervision of friar-builders. Furthermore, all the friar-builders were the product of essentially the same intellectual and artistic influences that made sixteenth-century Europe, and especially sixteenth-century Spain, a palimpsest of past and present. The elegance of Gothic, and behind that the vestiges of Romanesque sturdiness, the purism of the Italian Renaissance modified by the development of Italian and Northern Mannerism, the background of the Islamic (now Mudéjar) interwoven with Christian saintly iconography —all blended in these monastic houses.

The Franciscans in general built fairly simply because their first laborers were unskilled. Where skilled artisans were available, the Franciscans were especially fond of rib-vaulted interiors, as seen in part at Huejotzingo (pl. 6) and more consistently at Tepeaca. The Augustinians preferred more lavish carved stone façades and interior fresco effects, as at Actopan (pls. 24 and 26). The Dominicans, building in earthquake territory, tended to enlarge enormously the walls and supporting buttresses of their structures, as at Yanhuitlán (pl. 48). Though there was a slight over-all difference between the orders simply because, for example, the Franciscans' work preceded that of the Augustinians, who came to Mexico after the first waves of missionary activity were over, the technical and ornamental language of the period was a lingua franca that all spoke. The result was the creation of a group of monastic complexes which have similar features. Although the interpretation of those features might change from order to order, the basic parts were known to, if not used by, all.

Of first importance was a boxlike church, whose simplicity Kubler [2] has shown to be deceptively unlike either the classic Christian basilica or the ideal churches of the Renaissance. The monastic church, with or without a transept, was generally aisleless and devoid of flank chapels (fig. 5). A few churches were built with aisles (basilican type), with shallow nave recesses, or with deeper chapels creating the semblance of aisles exteriorly (what Kubler has called the crypto-collateral type). The choir or *coro* was over the entrance. Behind the altar in a polygonal, rectangular, or occasionally curved apse, generally without windows, was a great screen—a *retablo* or retable— carved and gilded, adorned with figures and ornamental sculpture and sometimes with paintings (fig. 14). Fresco painting on the plain church walls was the exception rather than the rule.

There was often rib vaulting in some part of the church roof, particularly toward the altar end of the interior; if not, a simple barrel vault roofed the church. Pier buttresses (flying buttresses were not common) provided visual confirmation of reinforcing at certain points of the exterior. The tops of the walls of the church were often battlemented. Sometimes there was a *chemin de ronde* or *paseo de ronda*, and usually the vaults were flat enough so that people could walk over their exterior surfaces. Kubler [3] describes the church with brevity and clarity: "The total effect is that of a battlemented church with simple and harmonious proportions, rising above the settlement in which it is the refuge, the citadel, and the communal center." (See also figs. 8 and 11.)

The church façade, like the great retable inside, was a principal focus

---

[2] George Kubler, *Mexican Architecture in the Sixteenth Century*, vol. II, chap. vi.
[3] Kubler, *op. cit.*, p. 232.

of ornamental enthusiasms. The main portal might be discreetly Renaissance, with a modified Gothic rose window above, or the entire
façade might be a distinctive mélange of Italian, Flemish, and Spanish
sources. Elongated Mannerist half-columns or broken Plateresque
columns (fig. 20) approximating types of sixteenth-century orders
(like the Classical Doric or Corinthian), flattened ornament rigidly
confined by a Mudéjar rectilinear frame (*alfiz*), angelic childrens'
heads (fig. 28), gargoyles, skulls, and crosses—a bizarre eclecticism of
parts enlivened these ornamental walls that never became more than
frontispieces to the simple buildings beyond.

The monastic quarters attached to the church, often unusually large
and elaborate for the number of monks to be accommodated, were
organized around a cloister, usually one but occasionally two in number, entered through an arched porch or *portería* and a corridor or
zaguán, at the side of the church façade. The monk's cells were aus-
tere cubicles, yet never devoid of a restrained harmony of proportion
or of the fitness of simple furnishings to the *vita contemplativa* of
scholarly thoughtfulness and the *vita activa* of conversion. In the arcades of the cloisters reminiscences of European monastic life were
most obvious—in the handsomely vaulted roofs, the carved capitals,
and the stone sitting and walking areas below, which invited the formal converse of a dedicated communal life. Occasionally black and
white fresco painting, closely related to the intense conviction of late
medieval woodcuts, decorated cloister walls or staircases, or illusionistic paintings of rosy coffered vistas enriched cloister or refectory
vaults.

The over-all plan (fig. 1) closely resembled the formal pattern of
the Early Christian church or more especially that of the Benedictine
monastic complex. Thus, the church was inevitably preceded by a
spacious courtyard (atrium or *atrio*), rimmed in Mexico with battlemented walls, which like those of the church were essentially decorative rather than defensive. In the center of the *atrio*, or in a separate
courtyard before it, there was usually a carved stone cross which,
more than any other single decorative-symbolic element of the monastic complex, revealed the persistence of Indian ornamental and
sculptural concepts. Even this rare survival of Aztec muscularity of
carving and the merging of Indian divinities with Christian was to dis-
appear by about 1580.

In certain of the monastic orders in which a more deliberate policy of evaluating the stages of conversion among the Indians prevailed, there were outdoor chapels of various types in the *atrio*. Some were intended for social or educational activities among the Indians (*capilla de indios*); some were used for celebration of the Mass, or occasionally for some special local cult (*capilla abierta*, or open chapel). These structures sometimes approximated a regular church presbytery, although often they were treated as a form of narthex or porch removed from the church. There is considerable confusion in the interpretation of the *capilla abierta* or *capilla de indios;* Kubler has the best discussion of the problems.[4] Especially among the Franciscans, who were more selective in their administration of the symbols of the faith and who perhaps had a more thorough understanding of the problems of conversion among a people still so deeply imbued with their old faith, there was emphasis both on open chapels and on oratories at the corners of the churchyard (*capillas posas*), which were used in connection with processions.

Most monastic houses (*conventos*) were the foci of new settlements, which the friars were instrumental in laying out into regular grid patterns. These were generally situated in the country, near old Indian ceremonial centers. Sometimes the local Christian communities, with a high proportion of Indian to European inhabitants, developed into important provincial towns; others are as isolated today as they were in the sixteenth century. Some monastic houses were built in Mexico City. The Franciscans had a particularly impressive community of churches, chapels, and monastic housing in the area southeast of the present intersection of Avenidas Madero and San Juan de Letrán.

After the first fifty years of architectural expansion, there was a period of consolidation. Certain of the orders (notably the Franciscans) had overbuilt, and the unneeded houses were transferred to other orders or converted to different uses. New orders came to the viceroyalty of New Spain after 1580: the Jesuits, the Mercedarians, and others. The particular importance of missionary activity was less immediate. Henceforward the Jesuits and Franciscans would explore the still unconverted areas of northern Mexico, into the present southwestern United States (Texas, New Mexico, and Arizona) and into Baja and Alta California (the latter now California in the United

[4] Kubler, *op. cit.*, pp. 320–337.

States). On this new frontier the problems of a monastic complex as the center of a self-sufficient community, of native materials and native workmen under supervision of the friars and priests, would be pursued with many of the same modifications of European sources as in sixteenth-century Mexico. The mission churches of the American Southwest and the Californias, however, were generally much simpler than the great monastic houses of New Spain, being often built of adobe rather than stone, and with more limited resources of craftsmanship, native and itinerant.

Monastic houses continued to be built in Mexico proper throughout the viceregal period, with special emphasis on nunneries in the eighteenth century, paralleling the European nunneries as polite retreats from social or marital problems. However, the general emphasis after 1580, and indeed from 1560 on, was upon the secular clergy of the town. The struggle for power between monastic and secular clergy continued, with the eventual triumph of the latter—more closely allied to the royal power of king and Spain, of viceroy and New Spain.

Cathedrals

The principal urban centers of Mexico in the viceregal era were Mexico City, Puebla, and Guadalajara. Morelia (or, as it was then called, Valladolid), Oaxaca, and the towns of the northern mines and haciendas (like San Luis de Potosí, Saltillo, and Monterrey) were secondary centers, eventually replacing the provincially important Pátzcuaro, San Cristóbal de las Casas, Cuernavaca, and others of the sixteenth century. (The towns of Yucatán are beyond the geographical limits of this book.) The principal focus of the urban center's religious life was the cathedral. The present Cathedral of Mexico (pl. 94) was planned in the later sixteenth century. The cathedrals in Puebla and Guadalajara were roughly contemporary, in their formative development, with the first stages of the Cathedral of Mexico. Construction was slow on these major edifices, partly because of costs and technical problems, partly because of procrastination and intrigue among the supervising juries of competence. However, between 1630 and 1680, the Cathedral of Mexico was structurally well advanced (the façade and its details, the tower tops, and the drum and cupola over the crossing were finished later); and Puebla and Guadalajara were virtually completed, although both were to be substantially revised at later periods. The Cathedral of Morelia was begun, although construction lagged for some decades after an ambitious beginning. The Cathedral of Oaxaca continued slowly on a sixteenth-century foundation; it was not to be finished until well into the eighteenth century.

Most of the northern towns had not yet sprung into the prominence they achieved later with the discovery of immense mineral resources and the large-scale exploitation of the agricultural and cattle-raising potential of that area. Their cathedrals were often parish churches converted to a higher ecclesiastic dignity in the later eighteenth, nineteenth, or twentieth centuries. A few of Mexico's present large number of cathedrals were converted from monastic churches (such as the Franciscan church in Cuernavaca), to suit the diocesan needs of a population vastly increased since viceregal times.

The essential fact remains that, after a period of transition from the ascendancy of the monastic clergy to that of the secular town clergy, the major cathedrals of Mexico were firmly initiated or were nearing structural completion by 1680. They represented a wholly different focus of artistic energies and a wholly different concept of planning from the monastic churches. Reverting in general to the basilican plan of western European Christianity, especially the cathedrals of the Gothic age, they were nevertheless special variants of the cathedrals of Spain. (Some of the early Mexican cathedrals were variants of the hall church.) Their interior proportions, their placement of the *coro* toward the entrance end of the nave in the Spanish manner, and their absorption of the planning principles of the late sixteenth-century Spanish architects put them in a special architectural group.

Since many of these cathedrals were founded in the late sixteenth century, they retained traces of late medieval stereotomy in their roof systems, which often were ribbed vaults that gradually moved toward the domical roof units preferred in the Renaissance and post-Renaissance. Their nave supports were generally a variant of the compound pier developed in the Gothic era, although most of these great stone piers were clothed in classicizing vertical half-columns. The complex system of massive isolated supports and vaulted roofs required a more subtle mastery of the principles of architecture than had been possible in the monastic churches of the mid-sixteenth century. In certain instances, the usual problems of building were increased by additional problems of site (as in Mexico City, where the watery remains of an old lake bed caused endless difficulties in the early stages of the Cathedral of Mexico).

The aisled basilican plan of the cathedrals (fig. 6) allowed increased numbers of persons to circulate within a large and complex space and mirrored the growing importance of the town populations in the later sixteenth and seventeenth centuries. The retention of traditional Hispanic features, such as the choir or *coro* in the nave with a processional walk (*via de crujía*) leading from *coro* to high altar, never gave the Mexican cathedrals of this era the visual thrust characteristic of those in France. However, such planning tended to give importance to aisle chapels, if they were part of the plan, and to emphasize the visual ambivalence between side and center, between subordinate but accessible altars and major but inaccessible high altar. To these essentially Hispanic Gothic qualities of plan were added the sixteenth century's double heritage of High Renaissance impersonal balance (certain of the cathedrals were conceived as centralized plans with four towers, two front and two back) and Mannerism's irresolute adjustment of balance and imbalance.

Mexican cathedrals and the Spanish structures from which they derived were ill-suited for the intense focus of the Baroque period. Their extremely mixed adaptation of planning sources made it virtually impossible for most of these large structures to be adapted effectively to the all-inclusive Baroque rhythms of large and small. Constant efforts were made to force some kind of visual and dramatic unity upon them with such special features of Baroque scale and bravura as a façade or retable (figs. 12 and 15). In general these features came in the eighteenth century rather than in the seventeenth. Between 1630 and 1680 the cathedrals were a full-toned statement of the triumph of urban over frontier life; they continued to attract the best talents of all succeeding eras. The usual end result of continued revision was, however, an ill-concealed attempt to impose personal monuments upon a large and complex building (fig. 9 shows a characteristic silhouette) which defied the cohesive coördination dear to the Late Baroque. The radical changes to the Church of St. Peter in Rome indicate some of the problems involved here. In Mexico such basic structural changes, or such monumental exterior devices as the Bernini colonnade for St. Peter's, were never effected. Thus the cathedrals lack the structural and stylistic coherence of either the monastic or the parish church but are instead fascinating, if uncoördinated, documents of vital changes of taste over as many as three centuries.

Parish and Pilgrimage Churches

The parish or priest's church (as opposed to the monks' church or bishop's cathedral) was both the spiritual and structural answer in design coördination to the dilemma presented by the cathedrals. Parish churches were built in increasing numbers throughout the later seventeenth century. The impetus to a lofty silhouette and a dazzling interior with gilded altar screens, related to a dramatic frontispiece or façade with twin towers framing the central elements, gradually developed also (fig. 13). The parish churches of the seventeenth and eighteenth centuries were essentially similar in plan, although the eighteenth century consistently added elements of emphasis to the neutral envelope of the nave. The narrow box of the sixteenth-century monastic church gradually became higher in proportion in the parish church; the height of façade towers and staged tile dome was especially marked in the eighteenth century (fig. 10). The sources of the monastic and of the parish church were quite different, and their spiritual "aesthetic" was essentially unrelated; yet both affirmed the general importance of a strongly rectilinear silhouette in general fabric.

Many of these parish churches were still devoid of flank chapels, but in plan (fig. 7) almost all of them had the wide, squared transepts and apse of the Gesù in Rome. Whether or not the churches had been constructed with interior chapels flanking the nave, a number of special chapels were added at this time, such as the Rosary chapels of the later seventeenth century and the *camarines* and Loreto chapels of the eighteenth century. These were usually adjacent to the church and were meant to be related, though not structurally integral, elements of a total plan.

The great age of the parish church was the period between 1730 and 1780. A formidable number of town and village churches were either built or reworked at this time. Santa Prisca at Taxco and San Cayetano de La Valenciana are excellent examples (pls. 117 and 155). Special pilgrimage churches appeared in the same era, although, as was mentioned in the Introduction, there were comparatively few pilgrimage churches in Mexico like the "staircase" churches of Portugal and Brazil, or the spatially audacious pilgrimage churches of Germany—again because of a general disinterest in certain Late Baroque concepts of space and plan. Attempts were made to create the equivalents of these churches at the sites of the great cathedrals. The Altar del Perdón on the back of the *coro* in the Cathedral of Mexico, and the Sagrario Metropolitano attached to the Cathedral (pl. 95), suggest approximations of a parish church in or near the cathedral, albeit with more specialized function. The cohesive Late Baroque organization of elaborate ornamented façades or frontispieces and great interior retables (fig. 16) was also added to the cathedrals at this time, as in the new façade design and the Altar (Retablo) de los Reyes of the Cathedral of Mexico.

From about 1730 to 1780, Mexico brought forth such a profusion of new or revised churches designed for the parish or pilgrimage population that the mind can grasp their quantity only vaguely. (Pilgrimages, were, incidentally, a significant form of chance association of the diverse levels of the now developed Mexican social structure of *criollo,* mestizo, and pure Indian which could be found in almost any community.) In this era of the *nouveau riche,* when a commoner might become a *marqués,* or a girl marry a man capable of eventually ruling a hacienda empire greater than the holdings of a European prince, the quick succession of a number of fashions was inevitable. All were touched, however, with that superb sense of ornamental zest and excellence of execution which had been developing in all the arts. Some of the parish churches were veritable museums of eighteenth-century fashions (as Santa Rosa and Santa Clara in Querétaro). If they indicate a lack of enthusiasm for the Late Baroque spatial adventurousness of certain parts of western Europe, they were still products of eighteenth-century finesse and ability to combine a wide variety of rich materials into a superb ensemble. Their qualities are deserving of a special effort in understanding.

For the modern traveler all these formal types of churches can be a revelation of remarkable proficiency in design and craftsmanship. Far from being "colonial," many of the buildings reveal a quality that can equal the most sustained accomplishments of Spain and Europe in the same period. Comparison can provide stimulating material for evaluation, but in the last analysis a special sympathy is necessary to identify properly with the accomplishments of viceregal Mexico, especially the later part of the era.

III

The Churches of Mexico
styles and fashions
of adornment

The plates of this book demonstrate the importance of the generalizations, discussed in the Introduction, for viceregal Mexican architectural and artistic history. They also reveal the wide differences of
building types, from the monastic complex through the cathedrals to
the brilliance of the parish and pilgrimage church. To understand
these variations fully, however, one must be aware of a sequential
pattern of stylistic phases or fashions in relation to the adornment of
exteriors and interiors of churches, which can now be differentiated
and analyzed.[1] Almost no aspect of Mexican viceregal art is more
troublesome than the nomenclature of style and fashion as it applies
to the enrichment of the building types discussed in chapter ii. Not
only has there been a lack of agreement about terms in the past, but
there is still almost no fixed formal vocabulary among the few modern
specialists in the field. Fortunately, there is somewhat wider acceptance, especially in parts of Europe and the United States, of the
changes in the terminology of art history over the last fifty years.
But some Latin American writers have still to understand the full implications of what is called Mannerism (both Italian and Northern)
and Baroque.

[1] The Glossary and the figures are especially relevant to this section; the figures offer
a simplified visual image of certain forms and compositions discussed here.

It has been common to refer to a part of sixteenth-century Hispanic art as Plateresque. This word, derived from the mixed ornamental sources of the Spanish silversmiths or *plateros* of the sixteenth century, has since been extended particularly to New World architecture and art of the same era. Although the artisans and designers of the sixteenth century in Spain tended to equate their work mentally with Classical antiquity, it is obvious that the peculiar mixings of Spain and the New World at this time were anything but purist revivals of ancient Greek and Roman forms, or of the ornamental parts of those forms. Some of these forms and parts continued to be popular in new contexts in succeeding eras.

Architecture and especially ornamental motifs in Spain after 1530 were of an unusual complexity.[2] Italian Renaissance adaptations of ancient Roman and Italian Romanesque forms and details were slowly assimilated in Spain. The fairly well-marked development of Early and High Renaissance in Italy proper was not easily transferred to Spain, with its more persistent enthusiasm for Gothic (particularly northern Spain) and for Islamic-inspired work (particularly southern Spain, notably Andalucía). There were occasional manifestations of specific High Renaissance influence in Spain and Mexico (as in plan for the five radiating naves of the Cathedral of Pátzcuaro, Mexico, never built), but much of the Spanish and Mexican architecture and art of this period was more *generally* Renaissance (and later, Mannerist); it lacked the subtleties of the relative degrees of Classicism and anti-Classicism of Italian design.

Gothic ornament as such in Mexico was of a fairly simple type. Crenelations or battlements (figs. 11 and 30) were common. Regular pointed arches used ornamentally were rare except in vault surfaces (they occasionally appeared in structural form in cloister arcades); variants of arches of double curvature appeared occasionally. Flying buttresses, partly structural, partly ornamental, were used on a few isolated buildings. In the sixteenth century, Mudéjar geometricism was confined to triangular or rectilinear frames about portals of churches or *posas*, sometimes approximating the *alfiz*. Mudéjar-inspired craftsmanship was seen particularly in the exquisite *artesonado* ceilings of carved and fitted wood, sometimes gilded (as at San Fran-

---

[2] Figures 25–36 provide a means of relating motifs from various sources to different centuries.

cisco, Tlaxcala, pl. 23), or in geometrically paneled doors, which appeared in variant forms as late as the very end of the eighteenth century. Cusped Islamic arches or depressed arches with no apparent support in the center were, curiously enough, more common in Querétaro in the eighteenth century than in the sixteenth. Still, the presence of Islamic conventions of rich, flat surfaces of ornament, generally confined to specific areas, was exceedingly important in the sixteenth century, even if Arabic inscriptions and the specific formal ornamental predilections of Moorish Spain were virtually unknown in Mexico.

Because of the fairly obvious Gothic character of parts of the church proper, however, too much emphasis has been placed upon Gothic ornamental enthusiasms in the so-called Plateresque; and because of often repeated instances of Mudéjar influence (numerically small), undue emphasis has perhaps been placed upon Moorish in the Plateresque. The ornament of sixteenth-century Mexico was essentially Renaissance (and later, Mannerist), drawing upon a vast source material assembled by the engravers of Italy, Germany, and Flanders. It was from these sources that much of the so-called Plateresque ornament derived. The heads of angelic children (fig. 28), the plates of fruit, the garlands (fig. 26), the coffers, the prismatic, unclassical columnar forms with swags, bulbous enlargements, and so on (fig. 20), were inspired by variants of Renaissance and Mannerism rather than by Gothic or Moorish.

In Italy it would be difficult to differentiate style and structure. Early Renaissance buildings had definite characteristics, from their plan to the lightest section of enrichment; Mannerist buildings were equally canonic. In Spain and Mexico there was not the same consonance of design and enrichment of that design. Thus the word "style" in Spain and Mexico might be better equated with ornamental fashion, since structure was not so integral a part of the whole enriched design. This factor will remain a constant in any discussion of style in Mexico; the basic concern is with ornamental fashions on the surface of buildings.

The figure sculpture of the sixteenth century in Mexico employed the same mixed heritage as did architecture and ornament. The influence of the late medieval masters of the Low Countries and Spain was very early apparent, with the necessary interpolation of surviving Indian features and the new Mannerist poses and elongation in figures, as in architecture. Craftsmanship was at a high level, with itinerant European masters carving major works. The consistent evolution of the polychromed wooden statue of colonial Mexico began at this time; the Indian world had a tradition of sculpture in various mineral materials, but Aztec wooden figures have not commonly survived. Mexican fresco painting in the sixteenth century was closely formed on graphic art models, notably northern (especially German) woodcuts. Painting on canvas in the mixed technique (egg tempera and oil, usually on panel) or in some variation of Venetian oil (pure oil on canvas) came later in the sixteenth century, with the arrival of such European artists as Simón Pereyns. Ornamental enrichment of both sculpture and painting, as in a great retable (pl. 7), often reduced them to dependent parts of a large decorative ensemble, rather than major independent art forms.

Some of the Renaissance-Mannerist purism of the late sixteenth century, as in Actopan's façade or the interiors of Cuilapan (pls. 24 and 65), formed a Mexican equivalent to the austerity of Juan de Herrera's work in Spain and has been referred to as Herreran.[3] This purism was not altogether a major fashion in Mexico at the time. However, it remained a forceful undercurrent in all ensuing eras and reappeared particularly in the mid-seventeenth and mid-eighteenth centuries, before its more academic reappraisal in the Neo-Classical era. The Cathedral of Puebla was probably the most obvious example of this fashion in pre-eighteenth–century Mexico (pl. 102). Its gray stone and white marble exterior with Renaissance-Mannerist ornamental details had the general restraint of Herrera's work at the Escorial; but, like the church at the Escorial, it began to manifest Baroque proclivities (especially in scale). These proclivities were carried further on the façade of Puebla cathedral (of a later date in time and style than the Escorial church), especially in the relation of minor and major parts. From 1630 to 1680 the tide of the new Baroque rhythmic adjustment of minor and major, of subordinate side to dominant central, swept over parts of every Mexican colonial monument. It was particularly apparent in the retables and façades of churches of the period.

---

[3] The term *Greco-Romano* is sometimes used in Spanish (see Glossary); this adjective defines such early examples of Mannerist influence as the façades of the palace of Charles V at Granada and the later sixteenth-century work of Herrera, which gave rise to the Herreran label.

Even at this time of Early Baroque developments, however, the ornamental language was still essentially Renaissance and Mannerist, rather than of a wholly novel type. The garlands became somewhat more profuse, the angelic hosts somewhat more numerous, than in the Renaissance. The strapwork patterns of Flemish and German Mannerism (fig. 29) appeared in great prolixity; frames of doors and windows had enlarged "ears," following Mannerist precedent (fig. 33). An emphasis on lavishness was, of course, by no means the principal characteristic of the Early and High European (Italian) Baroque, but rather of a Late Baroque which lead irresistibly into the caprices of the Rococo. The general solemnity of the Early Baroque appeared in the Cathedral of Puebla's façade; even the seventeenth-century parts of the façade of the Cathedral of Mexico were grave and classicizing. Intense amplification of sixteenth- and early seventeenth-century ornament, sculpture, and painting into a typical Late Baroque dazzling of the senses did not appear in Mexico until the eighteenth century.

The arts of sculpture and painting were developed with great vigor in the seventeenth century. Increasing conformity in an age of consolidation of faith produced two distinct tendencies in the plastic arts. First, there was an aesthetic exploitation of all possible devices to involve the spectator in the work of art. Secondly, there was a religious fervor which sometimes produced works of commanding spiritual power, if lacking the intellectual integrity of the sixteenth century's more introspective viewpoint. In the plastic arts, more than in architecture, there was an opportunity to relate to the conventions of Baroque thinking in European terms, since painting was deeply influenced by the internationalism of Rubens' Baroque formal expression. Throughout the period, however, there continued to be throwbacks to earlier ages and earlier influences, and the irregular development of painting and sculpture in the seventeenth century parallels the erratic adaptation of the successive waves of extra-Mexican influence seen in architecture. The sculpture of the seventeenth century, like some of the painting, tended to emphasize realism and a terrifying authority of texture. The use of actual teeth and hair, of glass eyes, and so on, was constantly criticized but continued into the eighteenth century in substitute materials that approximated the grim reality of the seventeenth century.

In architecture proper about 1680, an important columnar form of twisted shape became more obvious in both interiors and exteriors. Its exuberant contour, with implied movement, paralleled the postures of the figure sculpture and religious painting of the later seventeenth century and sharply distinguished it from those broken and prismatic columnar forms seen so often in the sixteenth century. This twisted column with Corinthianesque capital (called *salomónica* in Spain and Mexico, from its presumed use in Solomon's temple) was the architectural hallmark of the era from 1680 to 1730 (figs. 21 and 22). With it was associated a lush, Renaissance-oriented ornamental vocabulary of large and small details, all closely related to the contemporary Hispanic work of certain designers in Sevilla and of José de Churriguera the Younger in Salamanca. From the brilliant vertical excitement of the *retablo mayor* (1688) of Santo Domingo, Puebla, Mexico, to hundreds of lesser works in chapels, naves, and transepts of other churches, the *salomónica* reigned supreme.

The *salomónica* was not always, in Mexico, the twisted column seen in Bernini's baldachin for St. Peter's or in some Spanish work such as José de Churriguera's (fig. 21); it was rather a cylinder with helical carving, the whole covered with infinite variations of the vines, grapes, and other motifs of the European *salomónica* (fig. 22). This helical Mexican *salomónica* may have been partly inspired by eastern Spanish and Granadine sources, where the helicoid column was more common than in Sevilla and Salamanca.

Along with the general vogue for the *salomónica,* there continued an enthusiasm for classicizing columns or pilasters, especially in Oaxaca, where a particular type of angled façade, similar to the great angled screens of the sixteenth century, also appeared, as in La Soledad (pl. 83). Classicizing columnar or pilaster elements used for articulation were residually important all through the eighteenth century, and were particularly numerous in capital and province in the first third of the century.

The design of both façades and retables tended to be stereotyped at this period. The composition of a portal with a column or columns at each side, sometimes with the same elements repeated above flanking a second opening (as seen, perhaps earliest in art history, on the city gate of Miletus) already had widespread use in Europe and early viceregal Mexico. A single variant of it, with prismatic Plateresque columnar forms or Renaissance-Mannerist forms, had sufficed for the sixteenth century. Three variants, with the central variant larger and higher than the two side variants, had created the basic Baroque façade compositions of the later seventeenth-century Mexican cathedrals. A single variant remained the major façade and retable composition of the eighteenth century. Didactic relief compositions might replace the second-level window or opening, but the pairing of vertical articulative elements on the sides, with niches between each pair, was almost invariable (cf. figs. 11, 12, and 13, and pls. 156, 94, and 104).

To avoid some of the oversimplification apparent here, it should also be added that there were actually two basic compositional arrangements in viceregal Mexico. The wider type, already discussed, was common on major façades and retables; the other, a narrow stepped composition with the higher levels progressively narrower than the lowest level, was more common on less ambitious façades, and especially on side portals. The first type was essentially Renaissance Italian (pl. 24); the second was apparently more Islamic (pls. 38 and 79). There were, of course, combinations of features from both types on some façades and retables.

Contemporary with the later popularity of the *salomónica,* another architectural form was making its debut. The *estípite* (from the Latin *stipes, stipitis*) was destined to replace the *salomónica* in the favor of Mexican architectural designers. This bizarre form (fig. 23), of complex antecedents, became a veritable Neo-Mannerist order in eighteenth-century Mexico. Like the *salomónica,* it had a classically inspired capital, generally Corinthianesque, though by no means classical in detail. Replacing the spiral or helix of the *salomónica* was a curious collection of parts, which soon became invariable for the *estípite.* Below the capital came squared and circular blocks, sometimes covered with medallions. Supporting these blocks (which varied in number) there was always an inverted obelisk, revealing the ancestry of the *estípite* in the herm bases of antiquity and, particularly, in Michelangelo and the sixteenth-century Mannerists.

José de Churriguera the Younger did not generally employ the *estípite* on his work, preferring the *salomónica* or the classicizing columnar form. Unfortunately, error and custom have settled on him the parentage of a style referred to as Churrigueresque, which is most often applied to works utilizing *estípites.* The era from 1730 to 1780 in Mexico was dominated by the *estípite* and its mixed Renaissance-

Mannerist-Baroque ornamental vocabulary. If the term Churriguer-esque must be used for this era, as is commonly the practice among popular writers on Mexican viceregal art, it might at least, as suggested earlier, be called Mexican Churrigueresque to give it an arbitrary significance divorced from José de Churriguera's name and style. Some authorities, as noted, beginning with Gerardo Murillo (Dr. Atl) and continuing with George Kubler, have preferred the term Ultra-Baroque for this period.

Ultra-Baroque has the advantage of having an entirely different connotation from Late Baroque, and, as Kubler has said, it has the implication of *ultramar*. It also, unfortunately, implies something either technically beyond the Baroque, or the climax of the Baroque. The latter connotation is undesirable because the era of the *estípite* was a combination of Late Baroque and Mannerist features and design attitudes rather than a climactic phase of the general European Baroque, and because Mexico was essentially uninterested in many mass, planning, and spatial aspects of the European Baroque.

It has seemed more reasonable to refer to these troublesome ornamental architectural periods after 1680 in terms of their principal articulating element. The proportionately great importance of ornamental architecture after 1680 makes this reasonable. Religious sculpture and painting were often parts of a whole design for façades and retables—the principal architectural design foci of the period. Choir stalls, organ cases, and funeral monuments (*piras*) were also adapted to most of these fashions, as were religious edifices that were not churches. Secular architecture—beyond the limits of this book—utilized many of the same formal ideas. Thus, the *salomónica* age, era, or period would then refer to the time from about 1680 to 1730; the *estípite* age, era, or period, from 1730 to about 1770, and so on (see Chronology III). If personalities' names must enter in, it would be better to use the name of Gerónimo Balbás or more especially that of Lorenzo Rodríguez for the *estípite* age, for these men were instrumental in popularizing the *estípite* and its mixed ornamental vocabulary of prismatic Mannerist-inspired motifs (fig. 36) and curvilinear Renaissance-Baroque–inspired motifs (fig. 34).

All over Mexico, following especially the precedent of the architect-designers grouped about Lorenzo Rodríguez, there appeared *estípite* façades and *estípite* retables. These façades and retables were probably numerically the most important design phenomenon in eighteenth-century Mexico. Their variations were limitless in extension, although the elements were unchanging in part. The development of regional styles, exteriorly related to the particular stone of an area (as Oaxaca, Morelia, and Mexico City) was recast to suit the conventions of the new interior fashion in gilded wood. Certain provincial areas remained more indifferent to the *estípite* than did others. The classicizing column or pilaster was not entirely forgotten in the zest for a new mode. Twisted columns and classicizing columns were often used in combination with the *estípite* (pl. 93), as they had been in Granada, where Francisco Hurtado had reigned over a circle of younger masters whose influence spread to Rodríguez and Mexico.

It was in part from this area of Hurtado influence that there came yet another new emphasis in design, especially after 1770, and perhaps best explained as a contemporary trend in much of the Late Baroque of southern Italy, Spain, and Mexico. In Lecce (in the Italian Apulia), in Rome, in Zaragoza, Spain, and especially in Andalucía—to cite but a few places—there were sporadic manifestations of an entirely *ornamental* articulation replacing architectural or pseudo-architectural articulation by columns and pilasters. Above and below the niches that almost always occurred on church façades—usually at either side of the portal and framed with various types of columnar form—there burgeoned ornament to create what may be called an ornamental niche-pilaster (fig. 24). Sometimes these ornamental niche-pilasters advanced in multiple layers or "in echelon," emulating the shadow-pilasters of Michelangelo. Gradually they usurped the articulative function of the previously important columnar or pilaster elements, which as gradually sank back into insignificance (pls. 153 and 154).

In Mexico the emergence of the ornamental niche-pilaster or pilaster-niche [4] coincided with the rise to fashion of Rococo ornamental forms. It would be hard to date exactly the beginnings of all that tracery of *rocaille* patterns (fig. 35) which eventually appeared so prominent on retables, façades, and especially in the minor arts of the church in the later eighteenth century; 1765 and 1770 are convenient

---

[4] The order of words can be meaningful, depending on whether the niche or the pseudo pilaster is the more emphasized.

and approximate dates, although sporadic Rococo influence can be dated earlier. (Much of what appears superficially as Early Rococo, as in the exquisite organ case at Santa Rosa, Querétaro, dated 1759, is really a curious example of Baroque anticipating Rococo, tempting one to describe it by the combined form of these two coined terms—Barococo.)

In general, the various motifs associated with the *estípite*—particularly the *pinjante* (fig. 36), usually called *faldoncito* or *guantelete* in Mexico, and the down-turned spirals (fig. 34)—as well as the prismatic character of much mid-century work in Mexico, were now suffused with the scalloped shell pattern and streamer-*rocaille* band of the international Rococo. Particularly fascinating combinations of the *estípite* period and Rococo forms were developed in the Bajío area (notably Querétaro) and in nearby towns such as San Miguel de Allende (façade of San Francisco, pl. 144), Guanajuato (façade of San Felipe, the former Jesuit church), and especially above Guanajuato at San Cayetano de La Valenciana (pl. 153). Here, too, the importance of a particular kind of influence from the capital was to be noted: the absorption of Hispanic ideas in Mexico City, the creation of a circle of designers there about 1765, and the dispersion of both the ideas and the designers themselves to the immensely wealthy mining and agricultural centers of the provinces, especially of north-central Mexico. In these regional centers new syntheses of international, national, and local were effected.

The *estípite* died hard; it remained an effective ornamental, if not articulative, part of Mexican design until the mid-1780's. In the south of Mexico a provincial retable with *estípites* (pl. 52) is dated 1789. However, the supremacy of the *estípite* as an eighteenth-century fashion had passed by 1775 or 1780. From that time until the rise of the Neo-Classical movement, various nontectonic designs carried the ornamental implications of the Rococo to a brilliant climax of reduplicated flat surfaces, surcharged with an incredible but controlled variety of details. Certain of the retables at El Carmen in San Luis de Potosí (pl. 138) and those at La Ensenañza in Mexico City were among the most positive examples of the ecstasy of paneled, stuttering surfaces in this last great expression of Baroque and Rococo exuberance. Underlying all later eighteenth-century Mexican architecture was the intense focus and richly plastic order, with or without complexity of motif, so characteristic of the baroque in general. All façades and retables were planned to lead the eye to distinct points of emphasis. Light—both natural sunlight and an extensive repertoire of lanterns, torches, and candelabra of great refinement—continued to lend its drama to church exteriors and interiors by day and night. The almost incredible intricacy and mixed ornamental language of the period, however, reflected the taste seen in the copybooks of the eighteenth-century French and German engravers, and those works of the sixteenth and seventeenth centuries which underlay them.

In this later Baroque and Rococo age there were continued manifestations of an ability to mix a variety of fashions and ornamental sources in a single building which is one clue to Mexico's special mestizo quality, in the wider sense of that word. The magnificent retable series were not of necessity planned *in toto* to lead to a stunning climax in the *retablo mayor* behind the main altar. Often the nave or transept retables (today sometimes called *colaterales,* although in the eighteenth century all retables were generally called *altares*) were as fine, as large and lavish, as the *retablo mayor.* The façade or frontispiece of the church, although essentially another retable—in carved stone rather than in carved and gilded wood—did not inevitably follow the same ornamental persuasion as the interior retables.

Unfortunately, figure sculpture generally declined from the grave seriousness of the sixteenth century and the vivacious drama of the seventeenth century into insipid grace or morbid penitence. Religious painting took on much of the superficial elegance inevitable in an age of surface splendors, despite the growing ferment of intellectual and political liberalism. The eighteenth century was, aesthetically, an age of marvelous ingenuity in the ornamental and so-called minor arts. If the retables were peopled with wan and effete saints, too weary to do more than display their handsome robes, if the frescoes and canvases were hardly more convincing of religious integrity than a Lancret *fête champêtre,* there was glorious compensation in the resplendent ornamental sculpture of these same retables.

Indeed, it is unnecessary to underline the general craftsmanly consonance of all the arts in this period and their special application to ornamental architecture. Much of the surface enrichment of religious architecture was essentially a form of church furniture used for cult and symbolic purposes as well as to display the virtuosity of the artisan. That this emphasis on material luxury and elegance of effect eventually vitiated the lingering Baroque vigor of figure sculpture has already been mentioned. The figures were incidental to a gorgeous convulsion of carving, gilding, and polychromy which enveloped them; the carved niches and their ornamental surrounds were more important than the saints within the niches. Even in so overwhelming a sculptural performance as the façade of Tepotzotlán's San Martín (pl. 99), the faces and figures were but overtones to this Mexican version of a Mozartian symphony—with elegant parts combined into a sense-stunning whole. If painting was superficial in device and banal in saintly story, it nevertheless reflected the graces of a period when religion had become a social accomplishment rather than a compelling scholarly mission or a fervent devotion.

Almost with a sigh of relief, art passed from the involvements of ornament and life in the later eighteenth century to the relative calm of Neo-Classical taste. The change came about largely as Mexico's inevitable, if delayed, response to the vogue for the Neo-Classical which had started in England and France some thirty or forty years earlier. Despite the often repeated legend that Manuel Tolsá brought the Neo-Classical style to Mexico in the forty cases of antique casts which came with him from Spain in 1791, and which helped to initiate the "proper" training of artists in the new Academy of San Carlos in Mexico City, there had been a consistent undercurrent of classicism from the time of the later sixteenth century in Mexico. And the Mexican José Damiano Ortiz de Castro had provided Neo-Classical revisions for the upper part of the Cathedral of Mexico just before Tolsá's arrival and eventual completion of the cathedral (pl. 94). Thus it required but the dismissal of the now breathless magicians of the late Rococo, and the classicism of the Baroque emerged as the Neo-Classicism of antiquity, revived again.

From 1790 in the capital and from the later 1790's in the provinces, a wave of monochromatic purism swept the country. It was indicative of older tastes, however, that Francisco Eduardo Tresguerras' El Carmen at Celaya, the key provincial monument of the early Neo-Classical, was essentially a late Baroque French design, touched with the color of a Mexican tiled dome. Only with the early nineteenth century did a more archaeological Neo-Classical style gradually develop. The tall, dramatic silhouette of the eighteenth century still prevailed in Mexican church design; and as late as the mid- and later nineteenth century, San Felipe at Guanajuato (pl. 147) revealed a fascination with staged parts in its rebuilt dome, recalling the carefully graduated, staged towers of the eighteenth century. Elements of viceregal architecture and art survived Mexico's political and aesthetic revolutions to influence the more recent history of the country. It would be unwise, however, to see these influences as trends; they were rephrasings of tested formulas. With the timid eclecticism of nineteenth-century Mexican art as a foil, they merely reiterated older predilections of form and design.

As a vital principle the viceregal art and architecture of Mexico was effectively and basically changed with the political changes which began in 1810, when the priest Miguel Hidalgo raised his revolutionary standard at the parish church of Dolores. The craftsmanship and splendor of the later stages of viceregal art lingered here and there in the minor arts, but the major involvement of the whole artistic community in an age of consistently evolving fashion and taste had ended.

1. Zacatecas
2. San Luis Potosi
3. Lagos de Moreno
4. Guanajuato
5. San Miguel Allende
6. Guadalajara
7. Querétaro
8. Yuriria
9. Cuitzeo
10. Morelia
11. Tzintzuntzán
12. Pátzcuaro
13. México, D.F.
14. Tepoztlán
15. Cuernavaca
16. Puebla
17. Taxco
18. Tepalcingo
19. Oaxaca
20. San Cristobal las Casas

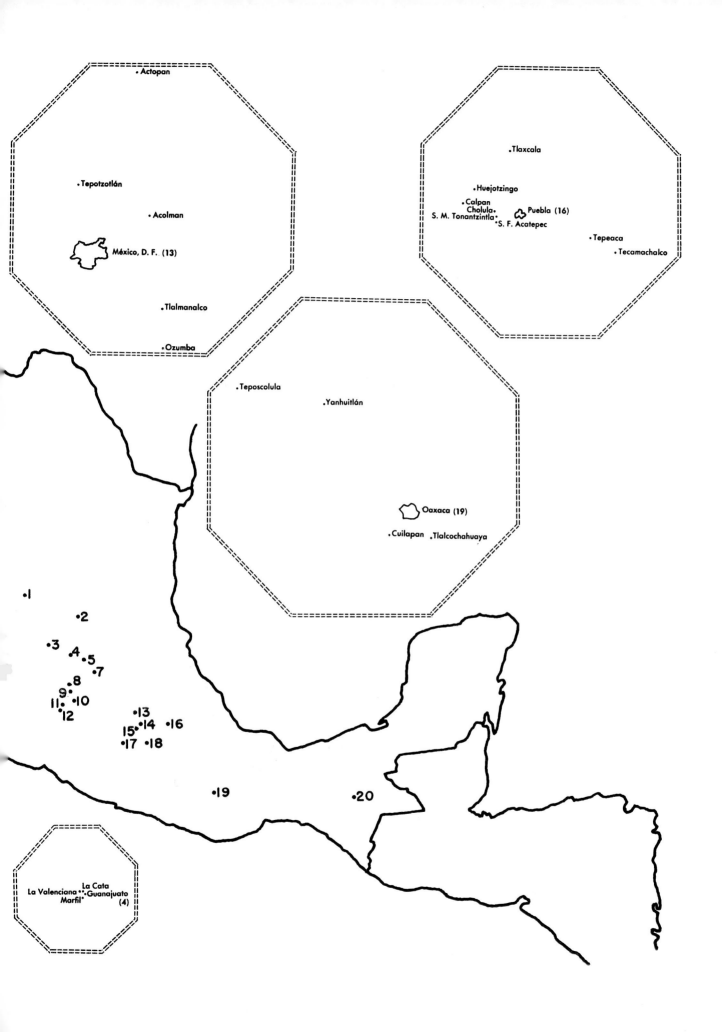

Actopan

Tepotzotlán

Acolman

México, D. F. (13)

Tlalmanalco

Ozumba

Tlaxcala

Huejotzingo

Calpan
Cholula.
S. M. Tonantzintla.   Puebla (16)
                    S. F. Acatepec

Tepeaca

Tecamachalco

Teposcolula

Yanhuitlán

Oaxaca (19)

Cuilapan   Tlalcochahuaya

•1

•2

•3   •4 •5
        •7
    •8
•9 •10
11• •12

•13
15• •14 •16
•17 •18

•19   •20

La Cata
La Valenciana •• •Guanajuato
Marfil•   (4)

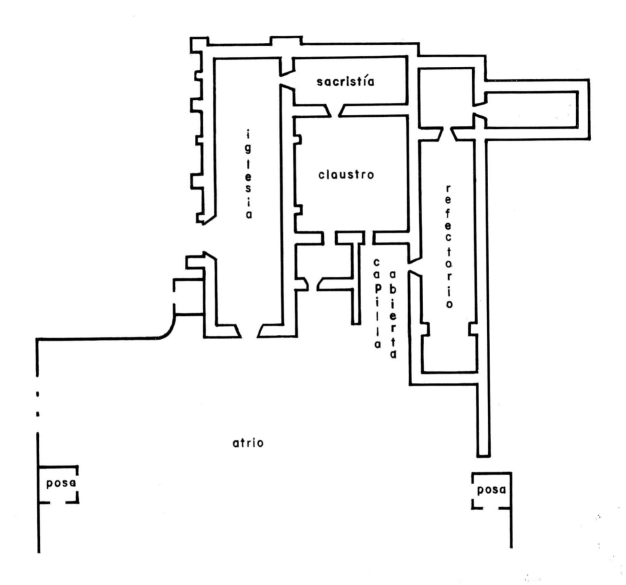

Fig. 1. Characteristic plan of a
sixteenth-century Mexican monastery.

Fig. 2. Franciscan
insigne: the stigmata's
blood and the cord.

Fig. 3. Dominican
insigne: the cross
of Alcántara.

Fig. 4. Augustinian
insigne: the bleeding
heart pierced with
crossed arrows.

TYPICAL CHURCH PLANS AND SIDE ELEVATIONS

Sixteenth Century

Seventeenth Century

Eighteenth Century

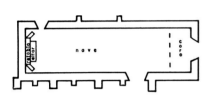

Fig. 5. Plan of a
monastic church.

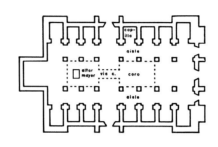

Fig. 6. Plan of a
cathedral.

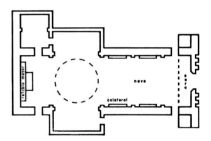

Fig. 7. Plan of a
parish church.

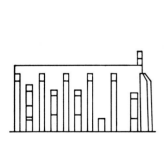

Fig. 8. Side elevation
of a monastic church.

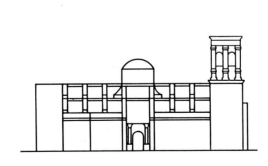

Fig. 9. Side elevation
of a cathedral.

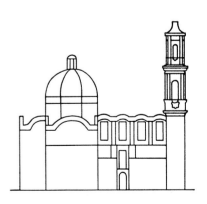

Fig. 10. Side elevation
of a parish church.

TYPICAL FAÇADES AND RETABLES

Sixteenth Century   Seventeenth Century   Eighteenth Century

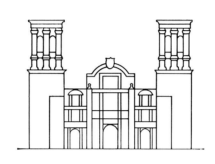

Fig. 11. Façade elevation
of a monastic church.

Fig. 12. Façade elevation
of a cathedral.

Fig. 13. Façade elevation
of a parish church.

Fig. 14. Later six-
teenth-century retable.

Fig. 15. Later seven-
teenth-century retable.

Fig. 16. Later eight-
eenth-century retable.

cornice

frieze

architrave

capital

shaft

base

Fig. 17. Doric order.   Fig. 18. Ionic order.   Fig. 19. Corinthian order.

SPECIAL COLUMNAR AND PILASTER FORMS OF SPAIN AND MEXICO—SIXTEENTH TO EIGHTEENTH CENTURIES

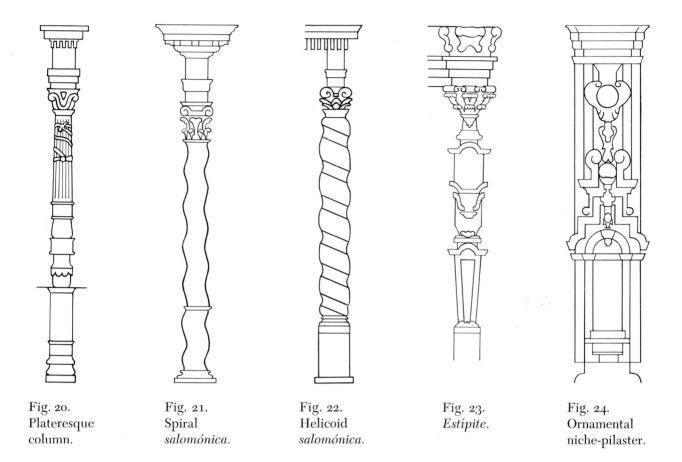

Fig. 20. Plateresque column.

Fig. 21. Spiral *salomónica.*

Fig. 22. Helicoid *salomónica.*

Fig. 23. *Estípite.*

Fig. 24. Ornamental niche-pilaster.

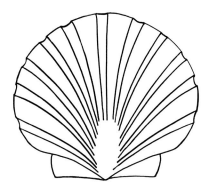

Fig. 25. Shell.

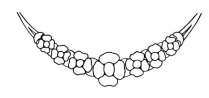

Fig. 26. Garland.

Fig. 27. Mudéjar paneling.

Fig. 28. Angelic child's head.

Fig. 29. Strapwork.

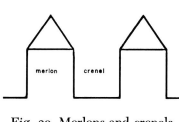

Fig. 30. Merlons and crenels.

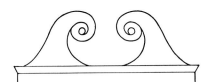

Fig. 31. Broken pediment.

Fig. 32. Rinceau.

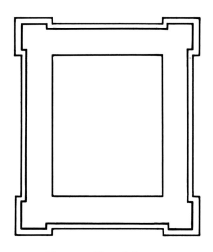

Fig. 33. Eared frame.

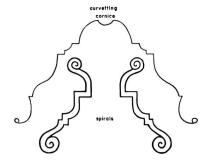

Fig. 34. Opposed down-turned spirals and cur-vetting cornice.

Fig. 35. *Rocaille*.

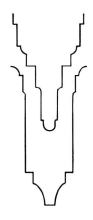

Fig. 36. *Pinjante*.

General

Sixteenth
century

Figures 25–36 are arranged to present some visual pattern of motifs which were persistent throughout the viceregal era, or were especially characteristic of one of the great building centuries. The arrangement is personal to the author, and is not meant to suggest that such a scheme actually prevailed in the minds of designers. Furthermore, the limitations of space have permitted only a few of the most important motifs to be illustrated; a special study could well be written on this subject alone. A few of the major secondary sources of ornamental history are listed in the Bibliography.

Figures are scaled individually, especially certain of the plans and elevations.

Seventeenth
century

Eighteenth
century

CHRONOLOGIES

The following three chronologies are approximate in date. It is impossible to suggest accurately the progressive and conservative phases of any period in so short a survey, nor is it possible to imply the relative importance of certain areas. The Renaissance, for example, was early and importantly developed in Tuscany, Italy; it did not have any major relevance to England, France, or Spain until much later. For the West in general and Spain in particular, the chronologies are in terms of centuries, with some specific dating where it has seemed meaningful. For Mexico, a more exact chronology is desirable, in order to relate to the text of the book. This chronology too must be interpreted as an approximation, since within any given country there was considerable variation from area to area in the adaptation of new ideas and fashions. The following general scheme was used in assigning periods to any given century: early, first third of century; mid-, second third; late, last third.

Architecture and Art of the Western World
from Late Roman to Neo-Classical

Late Roman and Early Christian	Third to sixth century A.D.
Medieval	Sixth to fifteenth century (and early sixteenth century in northern Europe)
Barbarian kingdoms—"Dark Ages"	Sixth to ninth
Carolingian and Pre-Romanesque	Ninth to tenth
Romanesque	Tenth to mid-twelfth
Gothic	Mid-twelfth to fifteenth (and early sixteenth in northern Europe)
Renaissance	Fifteenth to mid-sixteenth century
Mannerist	Mid- and late sixteenth century
Baroque	Seventeenth and early eighteenth century
Rococo	Mid-eighteenth century
Neo-Classical	Late eighteenth and early nineteenth century

CHRONOLOGY II

Spanish Architecture and Art
from Medieval to Neo-Classical

Moorish (Islamic influence in southern Spain)	Ninth to late fifteenth century
Gothic (especially in northern Spain)	Thirteenth to mid-sixteenth century
Plateresque (combinations of Gothic and Renaissance, with some Mudéjar features)	Late fifteenth to mid-sixteenth century
Greco-Romano and Herreran (variants of the Mannerist style)	Mid- to late sixteenth century
Baroque and Rococo	Seventeenth to late eighteenth century
Baroque developments, with emphasis on the twisted column or *salomónica* in façades and retables	1650 to 1720
Late Baroque, with Mannerist-inspired features (the *estípite*) in architecture	1720 to 1760
Late Baroque, with Rococo developments	1760 to 1780–1790 (earlier in Catalonia)
Neo-Classical	Late eighteenth and early nineteenth century

CHRONOLOGY III

Mexican Architecture and Art
from 1530 to 1810

Gothic survivals and Plateresque	1530 to 1580 (Conquest of Aztec empire, 1521; new period of building began effectively about 1530)
Herreran and Early Baroque	1580 to 1630
Assimilation of Baroque	1630 to 1680
Baroque developments * (*salomónica* era in architecture)	1680 to 1730
Late Baroque with Mannerist-inspired features (*estípite* era in architecture; particular influence of Lorenzo Rodríguez and his circle—the so-called Mexican Churrigueresque or Ultra-Baroque)	1730 to 1770–1780
Late Baroque with Rococo developments (ornamental niche-pilaster era in architecture)	1770–1780 to 1790
Neo-Classical	1790 to 1810 and later

---

* The use of *salomónicas* began before 1680 and continued into the *estípite* era; the use of *estípites* continued into the ornamental niche-pilaster era, as late as 1790. Rococo-inspired interior motifs appeared as early as the 1760's. The Neo-Classical began as early as 1780.

BIOGRAPHIES OF ARCHITECTS

BALBÁS, GERÓNIMO (*ca.* 1670–*ca.* 1760). Although documentation of Balbás' life is slight, it seems probable that he was born in southern Spain and died in Mexico. His fame in Spain was based on a large retable he did for the Sagrario of Sevilla Cathedral (later replaced). He may have worked in Cádiz (San Lorenzo) on smaller retable projects before coming to Mexico. Here he virtually duplicated his great Sevillian retable in the Altar (Retablo) de los Reyes for Mexico City Cathedral (1718–1737; gilded in 1743). He was associated with numerous other ecclesiastic projects in Mexico City, and even styled himself an engineer. Balbás adapted the *salomónica* retable of the late seventeenth century in Spain to the *estípite* fashion of the eighteenth century; unlike Lorenzo Rodríguez, however, he did not reduce the deep cave of space of this retable to a planar design. His works in both Spain and Mexico require further and more exacting research. The name is spelled variously—Balbas, Balbáz, and Barbás.

CHURRIGUERA, JOSÉ THE YOUNGER (or José Benito Churriguera, 1665–1725). The Churriguera family came from Catalonia to central Spain in the seventeenth century. In Madrid, Salamanca, and Segovia they dominated the architectural scene for two decades, although by the early eighteenth century dynastic changes in the royal house brought their competitors to prominence. José Benito was leader of the family after 1684. His mature work was concentrated on large retable projects (the Sagrario of Segovia Cathedral, 1686–1690, and the *retablo mayor* for San Esteban, Salamanca, 1693), with great *salomónicas* articulating curved spaces. In late life he turned more specifically to architecture, designing the model town of Nuevo Baztán for Goyeneche in a severely purist style of architecture, reminiscent of Herrera. There is little in either his retable or building design to relate to the word "Churrigueresque" as it is currently used.

Churrigueresque was the product of Andalusian designers rather than those of central and northwestern Spain.

HERRERA, JUAN DE (*ca.* 1530–1597). Herrera early accompanied Philip II to Italy and Flanders. By 1563, he was the assistant of Juan Bautista de Toledo in his work on the Escorial. After 1572 he became more intimately involved in this enormous palace-monastery near Madrid, and was responsible for reorganizing the workshops and completing the roofs, as well as adding to the west façade. His main design contributions were in the Escorial church (1574–1582) and infirmary. He worked on the royal residence of Aranjuez (after 1567), on the Exchange in Sevilla (after 1582), and on the Cathedral of Valladolid (after 1585). His style was based on a meticulous adjustment of mathematics and severely considered masses, with sparing use of ornament—classicist in conception and Mannerist in effect.

HURTADO, FRANCISCO (1669–1725). Francisco Hurtado Izquierdo y Fernández was the leading architect of Granada in the early years of the eighteenth century. His earliest work appears to have been a *camarín* for Malaga; but his style matured especially at the Carthusian house in Granada, where he designed the Sagrario and probably initiated the sacristy. The richly plastic effects of the Sagrario are apparent in his late project for El Paular, near Segovia (unfinished at his death, and completed by pupils). In Granada he was occupied with important retable commissions, including the influential retable of Santiago in Granada Cathedral, where the *estípite* appears in the form of salient pilasters. Hurtado's genius created a number of new configurations, including particular emphasis on the upper center of retables through "pushed-up" cornices and silhouetted figures. He was the focus of a large school of designer-architects, and undoubtedly had much to do, indirectly, with developments of the mid-eighteenth century in Mexico.

RODRÍGUEZ, LORENZO (1704–1774). Son of an architect from Córdoba and a woman from Guadix, near Granada, Lorenzo Rodríguez united the traditions of those two areas in his later work, although the actual amount of experience he may have had in Spain is still unknown. He claimed important positions at Cádiz, but his first work in Mexico (in the 1730's) was in carpentry at the Mint. After marrying the niece of a prominent architect, he inherited both the problems and prestige of the older man. From 1740 on he became the leading figure of Mexico City, and was involved in almost every important project of the time. Aside from the Sagrario Metropolitano (1749–1768), on which he worked largely between 1750 and 1760, Rodríguez designed residences, chapels, church façades, and numerous other works, which are yet to be fully documented. Certain longstanding popular attributions to him (such as the Tepotzotlán façade and that of La Santísima in Mexico City) seem dubious from stylistic evidence. His principal contribution lay in popularizing the retable-façade and developing it into a Mexican formula that proved of unusual influence between 1760 and 1780, especially.

TOLSÁ, MANUEL (1757–1816). Born at Enguerra, Spain, Tolsá was educated at the Academy of nearby Valencia. He arrived in Mexico City in 1791, well recommended, and assumed the positions of *maestro mayor* of the Cathedral and director of sculpture at the recently founded Academy of San Carlos. Although usually called a Neo-Classicist, Tolsá used Late Baroque scale and many individual elements of Baroque design in his work. He was architect (the Minería palace, 1797–1813 and later, is his most notable structure) and sculptor (the so-called "Caballito," or equestrian monument to the last Spanish king to rule Mexico, Charles IV, is his finest large work).

TRESGUERRAS, FRANCISCO EDUARDO DE (1759–1833). Mexican born and largely self-trained, Tresguerras became the finest provincial exponent of Neo-Classicism. Like Tolsá in the capital, his works show strong connections with the Late Baroque in their scale and in many parts. He finished sections of older buildings, designed a bridge and reservoirs, and found time to paint large canvases and to write poetry. His principal efforts were directed toward the embellishment of his native town of Celaya, where the imprint of his majestic style is still dominant. He did not, contrary to long-standing popular tradition, design the retables at Santa Rosa, Querétaro, since his birth date was not 1745 but 1759, or that even his early maturity was too late for the work at Santa Rosa. He was buried in a Neo-Classical temple-tomb of his own design, at the side of the church of San Francisco in Celaya, not far from the elegant church of El Carmen (1802–1807), his best-known building.

GLOSSARY

Adobe   Mud brick dried in the sun.

Aisle   Longitudinal space division of a church interior, generally at the sides of a central aisle or nave (*q.v.*) in larger churches and cathedrals; deep chapels may simulate the appearance of aisles exteriorly in cryptocollateral churches (*q.v.*).

Alfiz   Rectilinear frame, usually around an arched wall opening (door or window), often confining ornament to a delimited area (fig. 11).

Altar   Table for celebration of the Mass. Used in special sense (as *altar*) by writers of later viceregal period in Mexico to refer to a *retablo* or *colateral* (*q.v.*).

Apse   The polygonal or curved enlargement of the main altar end (traditionally, the eastern end) of a church to provide more space and emphasis for the altar.

Arcade   A row of arches on columns, piers, or pillars, usually carrying a roof, wall, or some other superstructure.

Architrave   Lowest horizontal division of an entablature (*q.v.*). Decorated characteristically for each of the orders and their variations (figs. 17–19).

Archivolt   An architrave or wide molding carried around an arch.

Argamasa   A cement-like composition substance, approximating stone in color and appearance.

Artesonado   Wooden ceiling made up of interlacing strips or sections in a geometric pattern; Islamic in origin.

Atlantes   Figures of human males, used architecturally or ornamentally as columns or pilasters.

Martin S. Briggs, *Everyman's Concise Encyclopedia of Architecture* (London: Dent; New York: Dutton, 1959) has a full listing of general architectural terms; the present Glossary is intended primarily to clarify special terms used in this text and Catalogue. Useful lists of Spanish and Mexican words and translations of Indian and Spanish place names can be found in Sanford, *The Story of Architecture in Mexico*, pp. 341–346.

Atrio   An atrium (*q.v.*) or forecourt (fig. 1).

Atrium   The space in front of a church, usually enclosed or raised on a terrace with the church.

Baroque   Style of architecture and art common to the Western world in the seventeenth and eighteenth centuries A.D.; sometimes divided into phases (especially in Italy) of Early, High, and Late Baroque. Usually characterized by a controlled organization of minor and major parts, leading to a dramatic focus of design elements, and often showing strong contrasts of light and color as well as movement of parts forward and backward.

Barrel vault   A tunnel-like vault.

Basilica   A rectilinear building, usually with a nave higher than the aisles; when used as a church, there is normally an apse, and sometimes a transept (*q.v.*). Also used as an ecclesiastical designation in the Roman Catholic Church.

Battlement   *See* Crenelation.

Bay   Compartmental division of nave, aisle, or other long space.

Buttress   A strong, projecting vertical support for a wall. May be a pier buttress (solid pier attached to wall, fig. 8) or flying buttress (arches brought from upper parts of building to piers at some remove from the wall).

Camarín   Special, small room for robing an image and storing its adornments.

Campanario   A bell tower, to be distinguished from a wall belfry or *espadaña* (*q.v.*).

Capilla abierta   An open chapel; the phrase is used loosely for certain structures of sixteenth-century Mexican monasteries, usually adjacent to the church. The true open chapel had provision for celebration of the Mass—a consecrated altar for the Host.

Capilla de indios   An Indian chapel; often confused with *capilla abierta* (and inconsistently used in literature of the viceregal era). A *capilla de indios* was generally intended as a gathering place for social or fiscal purposes, and normally did not have an altar.

Capilla mayor   The area directly around the main or high altar. *See* Presbytery.

Capital   The carved top of a column or pilaster (figs. 17–19).

Caryatids   Human female figures used architecturally or ornamentally as columns or pilasters.

Cathedral   A church that is the seat of a bishopric.

Cayola   *See* escayola.

Chemin de ronde   French phrase for an exterior passageway (*paseo de ronda* in Spanish).

Chiluca   Gray-white limestone.

Churrigueresque   *See* Mexican Churrigueresque.

Classic   The highest phase of any style or era of art. Sometimes used as a synonym for Classical (*q.v.*).

Classical   Ancient Greek or Roman forms, or directly imitative of them (as in Neo-Classical).

Classicist   Derived from Classical forms, but variously interpreted in a new context (as Renaissance or Baroque classicism).

Claustro   *See* Cloister.

Clerestory   The top level of a nave wall, with windows.

Cloister   Open court, usually with planting, surrounded by covered passages, in the residential part of a monastery. In Spanish, *claustro* (fig. 1).

Coffer   A polygonal, boxlike recess (often octagonal), frequently found in ceilings. Sometimes simulated in painting.

Colateral   See Retablo.

Colonnade   A row of columns.

Colonnette   A small column, usually very tall and slender in proportion.

Column   An architectural support of definite proportions, usually cylindrical in shape with shaft and capital (and sometimes a base). May be free-standing or attached to a wall ("engaged") as a half- or three-quarter column (that is, a column cut vertically in half or into three-quarters).

Composite   One of the Roman-Renaissance (and later) orders related to the Corinthian, but combining in its capital the leaves of the Corinthian and the volutes of the Ionic.

Convento   A Spanish word applied to both monasteries and convents, although generally to the former in sixteenth-century Mexico.

Corbel   A stone or wooden bracket, usually built into a wall to support a beam or vault section.

Corinthian   One of the principal architectural orders, originally taller than the Doric and Ionic, having a fluted shaft, capital with acanthus leaves and small corner spirals, and base (fig. 19).

Corinthianesque   Adapted from the Corinthian order, especially its capital.

Cornice   Topmost horizontal division (figs. 17–19) of an entablature (*q.v.*). Sometimes isolated and used separately as a strong molding.

Coro   The choir. Sometimes differentiated, in Spanish, as the *coro alto* (choir on an upper level) and the *coro bajo* (the area under the upper-level choir) in churches where the choir is placed over the entrance at the end opposite the altar, rather than being in the nave (as in certain Spanish and Mexican cathedrals, fig. 6).

Crenelation   A form of battlement, created in idea with indentations (crenels) of a low wall; in fact, often made by alternating squared blocks or merlons (sometimes with pyramidal tops), with embrasures or empty spaces between. Originally intended as part of the defensive wall of a fortress; in Mexico, crenelation was largely decorative (figs. 11 and 30).

Cross   One of the principal Christian symbols; architecturally, either of the Latin type (cross with one arm longer than the others) or the Greek type (with all arms of equal length).

Crossing   Area where nave and transept intersect.

Cryptocollateral church   A church, with flank chapels, that appears to be aisle-less interiorly but has a basilican massing exteriorly.

Dentil   Toothlike ornaments, in a row or "course"; originally associated especially with the Ionic order, but later with others also.

Dome   A cupola. A convex roof, usually circular at the base and semicircular or paraboloid in elevation (fig. 10).

Doric   One of the principal architectural orders; the Greek Doric had a simple capital with block (abacus) and curved "cushion" (echinus) over a plain, fluted shaft (fig. 17). The Roman, Renaissance, and Baroque Doric was closer to the Tuscan (*q.v.*).

Drum   A cylindrical (or polygonal) ring of structure on which a dome is sometimes placed to elevate it. The drum often has openings or windows for lighting the interior below (fig. 10).

Encomendero   A holder of a large crown property (*encomienda*) and especially of a labor grant in early post-Conquest Mexico.

Entablature   The horizontal section above columns or pilasters. In Classical architecture and its derivatives, the entablature is divided into three horizontal parts from botton to top: the architrave, the frieze, and the cornice (*q.v.*). Each of the orders had a characteristic entablature, with special decorative enrichment of the parts (figs. 17–19).

Espadaña   A wall belfry; that is, a section of wall, usually placed over the façade, with arched openings for holding bells (fig. 11).

Escayola   A hard stucco or plaster, similar in effect to *argamasa* (*q.v.*).

Estípite   Special pillar or pilaster made up of a base, inverted obelisk, various blocks and moldings (sometimes medallions as well), and crowned with a Corinthianesque capital (fig. 23). Developed from herm pedestals (*q.v.*) of the sixteenth century, and first used in a developed form in the later seventeenth century. Became a type of "order" in mid- and later eighteenth-century Mexico.

Estofado   Figural and ornamental sculptural technique, involving the coating of carved wood with layers of fine gesso (*q.v.*) as a foundation for gilding and polychromy. A special variant, relating to the faces and hands of figures, is called *encarnación*.

Façade   The front, or frontispiece, of a building.

Faldoncito   *See Pinjante. Faldoncito* means literally "little skirt." One word (especially used in Mexico) to describe the pendent motif common on retables and façades of the *estípite* era of the eighteenth century; it is especially appropriate to such motifs that appear to be derived from a fabric fringe.

Fluting   Vertical channeling (usually concave) of a columnar or pilaster shaft.

Frieze   Middle horizontal division of an entablature (*q.v.*). Decorated characteristically for each order and its variations (figs. 17–19).

Gesso   Fine plaster of Paris.

Gothic   A style of architecture and art, essentially of the mid-twelfth to late fifteenth or early sixteenth centuries A.D. Usually characterized by pointed arches of varied shapes—some high and narrow, others low and flat or depressed—but occasionally by arches of double curvative, or ogival shape. Buildings were often rib vaulted and had pier or flying buttresses.

Greco-Romano   A term rarely used, formerly signifying an early Hispanic variant of the Mannerist style.

Guantelete   *See Pinjante.* Derived from the word for "glove," since the motif, variously called *faldoncito*, lambrequin, or *pinjante*, is sometimes shaped like a pendent, stylized glove.

Half-column   *See* Column.

Hall church   Church with aisles the same or nearly the same height as the nave.

Herm   A bust of Hermes, usually on an inverted obelisk pedestal; in ancient times employed as a road marker and popularized again by Michelangelo in the sixteenth century.

Herreran   Later Hispanic variant of the Mannerist style—from the name of Juan de Herrera.

Iglesia   A church.

Ionic   One of the principal architectural orders (*q.v.*); especially characterized by its capital with large spirals or volutes at the corners (fig. 18).

Lambrequin   *See Pinjante.* Originally a scalloped or cut-out cloth ornament, used often in strip form under a canopy or a baldachin. Since many of the pendent motifs, especially in wood or stone, of the *estípite* era were derived from such cloth (or paper) sources, the term is used by some writers to mean that motif, although in its original use it implied a *row* of such motifs.

Lierne   An ornamental rib, used in later Gothic vaulting; a short connecting link between ribs near the ridge.

Linen-fold paneling   Carved wooden paneling, imitative of a regular folded cloth pattern.

Maestro mayor   The principal directing architect.

Mannerism or Mannerist   A style of architecture and art, now especially associated with the mid- and later sixteenth century A.D. Characterized by tension, ambiguity, lack of balance, crowding of parts, and a proclivity for elongated shapes. In building, ornamental forms were often used in a structural way, and structural forms were given a more ornamental role; functions were freely mixed (at least in appearance). In sculpture and painting tall, tense forms in divided compositions mirrored the emotional and other problems of an era of religious and political uncertainty and transition. The style is often divided into Italian and Northern (European) Mannerism. The former was both structural and ornamental, and was particularly developed in Florence, Milan, Rome, and other Italian centers. Northern Mannerism was more ornamental (emphasizing strapwork and so on) and was developed in Germany and Flanders. Combinations of the two affected Spain and Mexico, where Mannerist qualities underlay some of the Late Baroque and Rococo.

Manueline   A brief phase of ornamental architecture, originally localized in Portugal between about 1495 and 1520, during the period of the voyages of discovery under Manuel I, which lead to interest in marine and exotic motifs.

Masonry   Built of stone, brick or a similar material.

Merlon   One of the solid sections of a battlement (figs. 11 and 30).

Mestizo   A person of mixed ethnic background; usually one of the various combinations of Indian and European in the New World. By extension, art of mixed background.

Mexican Churrigueresque   A term that can be applied to the *estípite* era in Mexico. Usually (and erroneously) applied to all of the eighteenth century, and used pejoratively to condemn so-called "excessive" ornamental developments of that period. Like "Gothic," "Churrigueresque" was first used as an expression of critical contempt, by writers unsympathetic to much of the later seventeenth- and eighteenth-century architecture in Spain. It has no scholarly relevance to the work of the Churriguera family (the term Churrigueran has been suggested for their work).

Mixtilinear   Usually applied to the upper edge of an opening that has a broken line when seen from the front. An "arch" of a more complex shape than a semicircle or point, reflecting late medieval, Islamic, and Baroque interest in unusual broken, curved, and stepped rims of openings.

Moorish   Originally a Moslem inhabitant of North Africa; later, a Moslem in Spain. By derivation, the art of Islamic or Moslem North Africa and Spain.

Mozarabic   Produced by Christians under Moslem rule in Spain.

Mudéjar   Produced by Moslems under Christian rule in Spain; but by extension referring to a general interest in Moorish (Hispanic-Islamic) ornamental forms, especially those emphasizing geometric patterns (fig. 27).

Narthex   A porch or vestibule at the entrance to a Christian church.

Nave   From the Latin word for ship. The central longitudinal space or aisle of a church (figs. 5, 6, and 7). Traditionally (in medieval Europe) oriented west (the entrance) to east (the altar); in Mexico churches had many orientations. The nave is counted as an aisle in, say, a "three-aisled" church.

Neo-Classical   A phase of architecture and art, essentially of the late eighteenth and early nineteenth century. Characterized by a revival of Classical forms, with special variations for contemporary use; thus, called by some writers Romantic classicism.

Ogival   Arches of ogee or double curved shape. Formerly, and now erroneously, applied to all of Gothic architecture.

Orders   (1) In architecture, the basic columnar types of the Classical-oriented architectural world: the Doric, Ionic, and Corinthian of the Greeks, and the Doric, Tuscan, Ionic, Corinthian, and Composite of the Roman, Renaissance, and later eras. (2) In religion, the divisions of monks and nuns into special administrative units, as the Franciscan order, etc.

Ornamental niche-pilaster   A figure niche, with massing of ornament above and below, made into a quasi-pilaster or sometimes actually backed with pilaster shapes (fig. 24). Especially common in viceregal Mexico between 1770 and 1790.

Paseo de ronda   *See Chemin de ronde.*

Pediment   The low triangular space between the cornice of a roof gable and the entablature of a Classical temple; by extension, any low triangular shape, with cornice above and below, used to suggest this, as in a pedimented window.

Pendentive   A spherical triangle used as transition from a squared space to a drum or dome.

Pier   A massive architectural support; proportions not fixed.

Pilaster   A flattened columnar form, rectilinear in shape, always attached to a wall.

Pillar   A slender architectural support, usually rather tall. Sometimes squared or rounded.

Pinjante   A cut paper ornament, in its origins used to decorate for festival occasions. One of the words used to describe the pendent motif of mid- and later eighteenth-century Mexico, which apparently came from various European sources (fig. 36). The scalloped edge (lambrequin) of a baldachin or canopy is one source for this motif; others apparently include metal ornaments and cut paper, as well as designs from the graphic arts of the sixteenth century and later. For want of a commonly agreed-upon term for this special motif (particularly developed in a geometric form in eighteenth-century Galicia and in an elaborated form with spirals in eighteenth-century Córdoba, Spain), *pinjante* or lambrequin seem the best current choices, although *faldoncito* and *guantelete* (*q.v.*) have their Mexican adherents.

Plateresque   A style of architecture and ornament combining especially late Gothic and Renaissance elements, with some Mudéjar features.

Portal   The Spanish word (to be distinguished from the English portal or door) for an arcaded corridor.

Portería   The entrance to a monastery—usually an arcaded porch or narthex at one side of the church façade (fig. 11).

Posa   Or more exactly, *capilla posa:* A processional oratory (rarely or never a chapel) at each of the corners of some sixteenth-century Mexican monastic atriums (fig. 1).

Presbytery   The area within the communion railing of a church, especially reserved to the *presbíteros* or clergy, and thus called the *presbiterio* in Spanish. Often essentially the same area as *capilla mayor*.

Refectorio   A dining hall or refectory (fig. 1).

Renaissance   A style of architecture and art of the fifteenth and sixteenth centuries A.D. Characterized by harmony of parts, (symmetrical) balance, and clarity, strongly influenced by Classical sources. Sometimes subdivided (notably in Italy) into Early and High Renaissance.

Retable   The French and English word for the Spanish *retablo*. Also can refer to a shelf behind the altar in an Anglican church. Some writers use the word *reredos* in place of retable or *retablo*, both of which are employed in this text.

Retablo   From the low Latin *retaulus* (*retro-tabula*)—something "behind the table" or altar. Usually in Spain and viceregal Mexico a large screen (figs. 14–16) to enhance an altar. (The Spanish word *altar* [*q.v.*] was more commonly used than *retablo* in the literature of the viceregal period.) The *retablo mayor* is the screen behind the main or high altar; the *retablos colaterales*, or simply *colaterales*, are those behind the side altars. The word *retablo* can also (especially after A.D. 1800) refer to a small votive painting.

Rib vaulting   Masonry roof constructed either with a network of ribs and panels or with ribs as ornamental enrichment on the underside of a vault.

Rinceau   A foliate ornament (plural, rinceaux) (fig. 32).

Rocaille   By derivation "rock," but generally variants of shell forms with serrated edges and an irregular shape (fig. 35).

Rococo   A special stylistic development of the Late Baroque. It usually involved the elimination of the Classical orders and the creation of a special system of ornament, using *rocaille* forms and stressing asymmetry within certain delimited areas. Originating in France, it was importantly used in central Europe, northern Italy, Portugal, Spain, and the New World.

Romanesque   A style of architecture or art, essentially of the tenth to mid-twelfth centuries A.D., although persisting in variant forms later. Generally characterized by use of semicircular arches, extremely solid masonry construction, and heavy piers; often with relatively simple masonry vaults.

Rose window   A round window, usually with tracery.

Rubble   Irregular, rough stones.

Rustication   Construction of stone or stonelike materials in which the joints are emphasized, usually in a regular pattern of beveled edges and often with roughened surfaces, approximating heavy stone blocks in layers.

Sacristía   A sacristy, or room for robing the clergy (fig. 1).

Sagrario   Building where the consecrated host is kept—often a kind of parish church for a cathedral.

Salomónica   A Solomonic column—that is, one with a twisted shaft, usually with a Corinthianesque capital, grape and vine (or foliate) covered twists, and a base. So called from the presumed use of such columns in Solomon's temple; columns of various periods now in St. Peter's in Rome are variants of the original type.

Shaft   Section of a column or pilaster between capital and base (figs. 17–19).

Staged tower   *See* Tower.

Stereotomy   Stone cutting for vault surfaces.

Strapwork   Interlacing flat bands or straps, often with curved edges; derived from ornamental patterns of northern Europe in the sixteenth century (fig. 29).

Tecali   Called alabaster, but actually a Mexican metamorphic stone (onyx).

Teocalli   A pre-Conquest pyramid (and temple).

Tequitqui   Combining pre-Conquest Indian and early Conquest Hispanic art forms.

Tezontle   Reddish volcanic stone or pumice.

Tierceron   A roof rib coming from the springing of the vault (or its lower corners) but not one of the main ribs.

Tower   A high squared or rounded structure. Generally squared in Mexico and used singly or in a pair to frame a church façade. Sometimes built in levels or stages which diminish in area as they go higher.

Tracery   Patterns in carved stone in a window or door.

Transept   The interior space of a church (often a basilica) at right angles to the nave (fig. 6); where the transept intersects the nave is the crossing, which often has a domical covering higher than the nave or transept. Although traditionally (in medieval Europe) oriented north and south, it has many orientations in Mexico.

Three-quarter column   *See* Column.

Triumphal arch   The arch framing the presbytery or *capilla mayor* in a church.

Tuscan   Roman, Renaissance, and later variant of the Doric order (*q.v.*), with a very simplified capital, and use of a base rare in the Greek Doric.

Ultra-Baroque   Term applied by some writers (first used by Dr. Atl—Gerardo Murillo—of Mexico) to the *estípite* era or so-called Mexican Churrigueresque.

Vault   A masonry arched roof.

Via de crujía   Enclosed walk between choir and high altar of a cathedral (fig. 6).

Volute   A spiral, especially those spirals used in the Ionic capital (fig. 18).

Voussoir   One of the parts of an arch; the apex voussoir is the keystone.

Zaguán   An entrance corridor (generally of a residential building) coming from the exterior to the cloister or courtyard.

Selective Bibliography

One of the clearest statements concerning bibliography of the arts of the colonial period in Latin America is that in Kelemen, *Baroque and Rococo in Latin America*, p. 279. Kelemen's bibliography is as reasonably complete as possible for its publication date of 1951. Since that time, Kubler and Soria in *The Art and Architecture of Spain and Portugal and Their American Dominions: 1500–1800* (published 1959) offer a contemporary reappraisal of the artistic literature of Spain and her dominions in the New World, with a discriminating selection of the most important works.

Excellent general bibliographies for Mexico are to be found in Angulo, *et al.*, *Historia del arte hispano-americano*, Vols. I and II (in the sections relevant to Mexico), and in Wilder Weismann, *Mexico in Sculpture;* more specialized bibliographies for selected periods of the viceregal era in Mexico are in Kubler, *Sixteenth Century Architecture in Mexico* and Baird, "The Retables of the South of Spain, Portugal and Mexico in the Eighteenth Century" (Ph.D. thesis for Harvard University, 1951).

Any serious student of the available literature will wish to consult Robert C. Smith and Elizabeth Wilder, *A Guide to the Art of Latin America* (Washington, D. C.: Library of Congress, 1948)—a monumental critical survey of published works to 1942. The *Handbook of Latin American Studies*, prepared by the Hispanic Foundation at the Library of Congress, and published by the Harvard University Press (nos. 1–13) and by the University of Florida Press (no. 14 to date), continues the thorough critical review of all significant literature published since Smith and Wilder's *Guide*. Sections on Spanish-American art have appeared since no. 14 of the *Handbook* (14–21 by Harold W. Wethey; 22–23 by Joseph A. Baird, Jr.). The works on Latin America at the University of California were catalogued some years ago in *Spain and Spanish America in the Libraries of the University of California* (Berkeley, California), I, 1928 (general and departmental libraries); and II, 1930 (the Bancroft library). A large amount of new material, since received, is not in these earlier lists.

This Bibliography attempts to present a cross section of the literature particularly relevant to the title: *The Churches of Mexico: 1530–1810*. Books and articles most likely to be available to the reader are given preference, although some less accessible but important works are also listed. The basic division is between studies of architecture and art and geographical-historical studies. Within these divisions, material on Spain and Spanish America precedes Mexico, since this offers a more logical continuity of general background and special Mexican developments. Under "Geography and History: Mexico," some general handbooks and guidebooks which may prove useful to the traveler are included.

Under "Architecture and Art: Mexico," general studies of the viceregal or colonial era precede specific studies of the individual arts of architecture, painting, sculpture, and so on. Some crucial works, originally listed under Spain or Spanish America (due to their inclusive coverage) are repeated in shortened form in these sections on Mexico, since they often bear particularly on that country. A few picture books —with fine collections of plates and, occasionally, measured drawings but with dated or superficial text—are given in the section on "Mexican Architecture in the Viceregal Era." A complete listing of monographs and studies of special sites is impossible in this condensed Bibliography. Some of the most carefully considered and accurate of these special studies are listed in the "Sites and Structures" division of "Mexican Architecture in the Viceregal Era."

Architecture and Art

GENERAL WORKS

I. ARCHITECTURAL HISTORY AND STYLES

Brinckmann, Albert E., *Kunst des Barocks und Rokoko* (Berlin-Neubabelsberg: Athenaion, 1923).

Fletcher, Sir Banister, *A History of Architecture on the Comparative Method*, 16th ed. (London: Batsford, 1959).

Kimball, Fiske, *The Creation of the Rococo* (Philadelphia: Museum of Art, 1943).

Osborn, Max, *Die Kunst des Rokoko* (Berlin: Propyläen, 1929).

Pevsner, Nikolaus, *An Outline of European Architecture*, 6th or Jubilee ed. (Baltimore: Penguin Books, 1960).

Semrau, Max, *Die Kunst der Barockzeit und des Rokoko* (Esslingen: Paul Neff, 1921).

Wölfflin, Heinrich, *Principles of Art History* (New York: Dover, n.d.).

II. ICONOGRAPHY

Benedictine Monks, Ramsgate (compilers), *The Book of Saints*, 4th ed. (New York: Macmillan, 1947).

Künstle, Karl, *Ikonographie der Christlichen Kunst*, 2 vols. (Freiburg: Herder, 1926–1928).

III. ORNAMENT

Berliner, Rudolf, *Ornamental Vorlage-Blätter des 15 bis 18 Jahrhunderts*, 3 vols. (Leipzig: Klinkhardt und Biermann, 1925–1926).

Evans, Joan, *Pattern: A Study of Ornament in Western Europe from 1180–1900*, 2 vols. (Oxford: Clarendon Press, 1931).

Guilmard, D., *Les Maîtres Ornemanistes* (Paris: E. Plon, 1881).

Jessen, Peter, *Der Ornamentstich: Geschichte der Vorlagen des Kunsthandwerkes seit dem Mittelelter* (Berlin: Verlag für Kunstwissenschaft, 1920).

SPAIN

Angulo Íñiguez, Diego, *La escultura en Andalucía*, 3 vols. (Sevilla: Universidad, Laboratorio de Arte, 1927–1936).

Baird, Joseph A., Jr., "The Ornamental Niche-Pilaster in the Hispanic World," *Journal of the Society of Architectural Historians*, Vol. XV (March, 1956), pp. 5–11.

———, "Ornamental Tradition in Spanish Architecture," *Country Life Annual* (1961), pp. 82–87.

———, "The Retables of Cádiz and Jerez in the 17th and 18th Centuries," *Anales del Instituto de Investigaciones Estéticas*, Vol. 26 (1957), pp. 39–49.

Bevan, Bernard, *A History of Spanish Architecture* (London: Scribner's, 1939).

Camón Aznar, José, *La arquitectura plateresca*, 2 vols. (Madrid: Aguirre, 1945).

Contreras, Juan de (Marqués de Lozoya), *Historia del arte hispánico*, 4 vols. (Barcelona: Salvat Editores, 1931–1945).

Gallego y Burín, Antonio, *El barroco Granadino* (Granada: Universidad de Granada, 1956).

Gómez-Moreno, Maria Elena, *Breve historia de la escultura española* (Madrid: Dossat, 1951).

Gómez-Moreno, M., Verrié, F. P., and Cirici-Pellicer, A., *Mil joyas de arte español*, 2 vols. (Barcelona: Gallach, 1947).

Hagen, Oskar, *Patterns and Principles of Spanish Art*, 2nd ed. (Madison: University of Wisconsin Press, 1948).

Hernández Díaz, José (text), and del Palacio, J. (photographs), *La ruta de colon y las torres del Condado de Niebla*, Cuadernos de Arte, Vol. I, (Madrid: Instituto de Cultura Hispánica, 1946).

Kubler, George, *Arquitectura de los siglos XVII y XVIII*, Ars Hispaniae, Vol. XIV (Madrid: Plus-Ultra, 1957).

Kubler, George, and Soria, Martin, *Art and Architec-*

ture in Spain and Portugal and Their American Dominions: 1500–1800 (Baltimore: Penguin Books, 1959).

Lafuente Ferrari, Enrique, *Breve historia de la pintura española,* 4th ed. (Madrid: Dossat, 1953).

Lorente Junquera, Manuel, "Churrigueresque," *Encyclopedia of World Art* (New York: McGraw-Hill, 1960), Vol. III, pp. 608–614.

Sancho Corbacho, Antonio, *Arquitectura barroca sevillana del siglo XVIII* (Madrid: Consejo Superior de Investigaciones Científicas, Instituto Diego Velázquez, Sección de Sevilla, 1952).

Sancho Corbacho, Antonio (text), and del Palacio, J. (photographs), *Jerez y los puertos, Cuadernos de Arte,* Vol. II (Madrid: Instituto de Cultura Hispánica, 1947).

Taylor, R. C., "Francisco Hurtado and His School," *Art Bulletin,* Vol. XXXII (March, 1950), pp. 24–61.

———, "The Rococo in Spain," *Architectural Review,* Vol. 112 (July, 1952), pp. 8–15.

Weisbach, Werner, *Spanish Baroque Art* (London: Cambridge University Press, 1941).

SPANISH AMERICA

Angulo Íñiguez, Diego, Marco Dorta, Enrique, and Buschiazzo, Mario J., *Historia del arte hispano-americano,* 3 vols. (Barcelona: Salvat, 1945–1956).

Emerson, William Ralph, *The Architecture and Furniture of the Spanish Colonies During the 17th and 18th Centuries:* Mexico, Cuba, Puerto Rico, and the Philippines (Boston: George Polley, 1901).

Gillet, Louis, "L'art dans l'Amérique latine" in André Michel, *Histoire de l'art* (Paris: Colin, 1929), Vol. VIII, pp. 1023–1096.

Hanson, Earl P. (ed.), *New World Guides to the Latin American Republics,* 3 vols. (New York: Duell, Sloan and Pearce, 1945). Vol. I: Mexico, Central America, and the West Indies.

Journal of the Society of Architectural Historians, Vol. V (Special Issue on Latin American Architecture) (1945–1947).

Kelemen, Pál, *Baroque and Rococo in Latin America* (New York: Macmillan, 1951).

Kubler, George, "Limitations of Research in Latin American Colonial Art," in Elizabeth Wilder (ed.), *Proceedings* of a Conference held in the Museum of Modern Art, May 28–31, 1945 (see below).

Solá, Miguel, Historia del arte hispano-americano (Barcelona: Labor, 1935).

Wilder, Elizabeth (ed.), *Proceedings* of a Conference held in the Museum of Modern Art, New York, May 28–31, 1945 (Washington, D. C.: American Council of Learned Societies, 1949).

MEXICO

I. General

Anales del Instituto de Investigaciones Estéticas, new series (1937 and later) (México: Universidad Nacional Autónoma de México).

Fernández, Justino, *Arte mexicano: de sus origenes a nuestros diás* (México: Porrúa, 1958).

Kusch, Eugen, *Mexiko im Bild* (Nürnberg: Hans Carl, 1957).

McAndrew, John, "The Relationship of Mexican Art to Europe: Problems in the Field of Colonial Studies," in Elizabeth Wilder (ed.), *Proceedings* of a Conference held in the Museum of Modern Art, New York, May 28–31, 1945.

Moreno Villa, José, *Lo mexicano en las artes plásticas* (México: El Colegio de México, 1948).

Museum of Modern Art and Instituto de Antropología e Historia, *Twenty Centuries of Mexican Art; Veinte siglos de arte mexicano* (México: Enseñanza Objetiva, 1940).

Romero de Terreros, Manuel (Marqués de San Francisco), *El arte en México durante el virreinato* (México: Porrúa, 1951).

———, *Historia sintética del arte colonial* (México: Porrúa, 1922).

Toussaint, Manuel, *Arte colonial en México* (México: Imprenta Universitaria, 1948).

II. Architecture in the Viceregal Era

Angulo Íñiguez, Diego, "The 18th Century Church Façades of Mexico," *Journal of the Society of Architectural Historians,* Vol. V (1945–1947), pp. 27–32.

Angulo Íñiguez, Diego, "The Mudéjar Style in Mexican Architecture," *Ars Islamica*, Vol. II (1935), pp. 225–230.

Angulo Íñiguez, Diego, *et al., Historia de arte hispano-americano*, Vols. I and II (Barcelona: Salvat, 1945 and 1950).

Archivo español de arte y Arqueología, Vol. XI, No. 31 (January–April, 1935) (special issue on sixteenth and seventeenth centuries in Mexico).

Atl, Dr. (G. Murillo), Benítez, José R., and Toussaint, Manuel, *Iglesias de México*, 6 vols. (México: Secretaría de Hacienda, 1924–1927).

Baird, Joseph A., Jr., "Style in 18th century Mexico," *Journal of Inter-American Studies*, Vol. I (July, 1959), pp. 261–276.

Baxter, Sylvester, *Spanish Colonial Architecture in Mexico*, Tresguerras edition. 1 vol. text, 9 vols. plates; photography by Henry Peabody and measured drawings by Bertram G. Goodhue (Boston: J. B. Millet, 1901); Spanish tr. with abridgments by Federico E. Mariscal, Leon Felipe, and Manuel Toussaint (México: Bellas Artes, 1934).

Berlin, Heinrich, "Three Master Architects in New Spain," *Hispanic American Historical Review*, Vol. XXVII (1947), pp. 375–383.

Carreño, Alberto, *La arquitectura y la ingeniería colonial* (México, 1918).

Cortés, Antonio, and García, Genaro, *La arquitectura en México; iglesias* (México: Museo Nacional, 1914). (Second vol. listed under Mariscal.)

Edificios coloniales artísticos e históricos de la República mexicana que han sido declarados monumentos (México: Instituto Nacional de Antropología e Historia, Dirección de Monumentos Coloniales, 1939).

Fernández, Justino (ed.), *Catálogo de construcciones religiosas del estado de Hidalgo*, 2 vols. (México: Dirección General de Bienes Nacionales, Comisión de Inventarios de la Primera Zona, 1940–1942).

Flores Guerrero, Raúl, *Las capillas posas de México* (México: Ediciones Mexicanas, 1951).

Gante, Pablo C. de, *La arquitectura México en el siglo XVI* (México: Porrúa, 1954).

Kelemen, Pál, *Baroque and Rococo in Latin America*. Especially chaps. 2, 3, and 6.

Kubler, George, "Art and Architecture of Mexico," in *New World Guides to the Latin American Republics*, Vol. 1 (New York: Duell, Sloan and Pearce, 1943).

———, *Mexican Architecture in the 16th Century*, 2 vols. (New Haven: Yale University Press, 1948).

Kubler, George, in George Kubler and Martin Soria, *Art and Architecture in Spain and Portugal and Their American Dominions: 1500–1800*. Especially pp. 69–82.

Louchheim, Aline B., "*The Church Façades of Lorenzo Rodríguez: A Focal Point for the Study of Mexican Churrigueresque Architecture*," Master's thesis, New York University, Institute of Fine Arts, 1941.

McAndrew, John, "Fortress Monasteries?" *Anales del Instituto de Investigaciones Estéticas*, Vol. VI (1955), pp. 31–38.

———, *The Open-Air Churches of New Spain* (Cambridge, Mass.: Harvard University Press, in press).

MacGregor, Luis, *El plateresco en México* (México: Porrúa, 1954).

Mariscal, Federico E., *La arquitectura en México: iglesias* (México: Museo Nacional, 1932).

México, Dirección de Monumentos Coloniales, *Three Centuries of Mexican Colonial Architecture* (in English and Spanish) (New York: D. Appleton-Century, 1933; México: Talleres Gráficos de la Nación, 1933).

Neumeyer, Alfred, "The Indian Contribution to Architectural Decoration in Spanish Colonial America," *Art Bulletin*, Vol. XXX (1948), pp. 104–121.

Sanford, Trent Elwood, *The Story of Architecture in Mexico* (New York: Norton, 1947).

Toussaint, Manuel, *Paseos coloniales* (México: Imprenta Universitaria, 1939).

———, "Supervivencias góticas en la arquitectura mexicana del siglo XVI," *Archivo español de arte y arqueología*, Vol. XI (1935), pp. 47–66.

Villegas, Victor Manuel, *El gran signo formal del barroco; ensayo histórico del apoyo estípite* (México: Imprenta Universitaria, 1956).

Wagner, Max Leopold, "Die Spanische Kolonialarchitektur in Mexico," *Zeitschrift für Baukunst*, Vol. XXVI (1915), pp. 249–263.

Wells Henry W., "Riches and Severity: An Episode in Mexican Architecture," *Texas Quarterly*, Vol. II (Spring, 1959), pp. 172–180.

A. PICTURE BOOKS ON MEXICAN ARCHITECTURE

Ayres, Atlee B., *Mexican Architecture; Domestic, Civil, and Ecclesiastical* (New York: Helburn, 1926).

Bossom, Alfred Charles, *An Architectural Pilgrimage in Old Mexico* (New York: Scribner's, 1924).

Brehme, Hugo, *Mexiko—Baukunst, Landschaft, Volksleben* (Berlin: Wasmuth, 1925).

Kilham, Walter H., *Mexican Architecture of the Vice-Regal Period* (New York: Longmans, Green, 1927).

La Baume, Louis, and Papin, William Booth, *The Picturesque Architecture of Mexico* (New York: Architectural Book, 1915).

Palacios, Enrique Juan, *Iglesias mexicanas* (México: Müller, 1920).

Van Pelt, Garrett, Jr., *Old Architecture of Southern Mexico* (Cleveland: Jansen, 1926).

Vhay, Anna L. M., and David, *Architectural Byways in New Spain: Mexico* (New York: Architectural Book, 1939).

B. SITES AND STRUCTURES

General

Benítez, José R., *Las catedrales de Oaxaca, Morelia y Zacatecas* (México: Talleres Gráficos de la Nación, 1934).

Cervantes, Enrique A., Photographic albums on Taxco (1928); Cuernavaca (1929); Morelia (1930); Oaxaca (1932); Puebla (1933); Querétaro (1934); Guanajuato (1937) (Mexico: M. Casas).

Specific

Acolman:

Official Guide (Instituto Nacional de Antropología e Historia, México, n.d.).

Calders, P. (text and photos) and Tisner and P. Calders (drawings), *Acolman* (México: Atlante, 1945).

Actopan:

MacGregor, Luis, *Actopan, Memorias no. 4 del Instituto Nacional de Antropología e Historia* (Mexico: Instituto Nacional de Antropología e Historia, Secretaría de Educación Pública, 1955).

Cholula:

Maza, Francisco de la, *La ciudad de Cholula y sus iglesias* (México: Imprenta Universitaria, 1959).

Guadalajara:

Cornejo Franco, José, *Gvadalaxara colonial* (Guadalajara: Cámera Commercial, 1938).

Guanajuato:

Septien y Septien, Manuel (ed.), *Razgo breve de la grandeza guanajuateña*, 2nd ed., prologo de Gonzalo Obregón (México: Academia Literaria [Col. de Joyas de Bibliográficas Mexicanas], 1957). Reprint of 1767 edition.

Huejotzingo:

García Granados, Rafael, and MacGregor, Luis, *Huejotzingo: La ciudad y el convento franciscano* (México: Secretaría de Educación Pública, 1934).

La Valenciana:

Cortés, Antonio, *La Valenciana* (México: Secretaría de Educacion Pública, 1933).

México, D. F.:

Alvarez Cortona, M., and le Duc, Alberto, "Sagrario de México," *Archivo Español de Arte y Arqueología*, Vol. XI (1935); pp. 97–101.

"Cathedral of Mexico," special issue of *Artes de México*, Vol. 32 (1960).

Collier, Margaret, "The Sagrario of Lorenzo Rodríguez," Ph.D. thesis, Yale University, in process.

Iglesias y conventos de la ciudad de México, 2nd ed., corrected (México: Secretaría de Educación Pública, 1934).

Toussaint, Manuel, *La catedral de México y el Sagrario Metropolitano* (México: Comisión Diocesana de Orden y Decoro, 1948).

Morelia:

González Herrejón, Salvador, "Morelia (Antigua Valladolid)," *Cuadernos Médicos*, Vol. II (April, 1957), pp. 55–70.

Liaño Pacheco, Ana, "La catedral de Morelia," *Arte en América y Filipinas*, Vol. I (1936), pp. 95–123.

Oaxaca:

García Granados, Rafael, and MacGregor, Luis, *La ciudad de Oaxaca* (México: Talleres Gráficos de la Nación, 1933).

Toussaint, Manuel, *Oaxaca* (Mexico: Editorial Cultura, 1926).

Puebla:

Maza, Francisco de la, "La decoración simbólica de la Capilla del Rosario de Puebla," *Anales del Instituto de Investigaciones Estéticas*, Vol. VI, no. 23 (1955), pp. 5–29.

Toussaint, Manuel, *La catedral y las iglesias de Puebla* (México: Porrúa, 1954).

San Luis de Potosí:

Meade, Joaquin, *Guía de San Luis de Potosí* (in English and Spanish), 2nd ed. (Mexico: Robredo y Rosell, 1946).

San Miguel de Allende:

Maza, Francisco de la, *San Miguel de Allende: su historia, sus monumentos* (México: Instituto de Investigaciones Estéticas, 1939).

Taxco:

Toussaint, Manuel, *Taxco* (México: Publicaciones de la Secretaría de Hacienda, 1931).

Tepalcingo:

Reyes Valerio, Constantino, *Tepalcingo* (México: Instituto Nacional de Antropología e Historia, 1960).

Tepotzotlán:

Gante, Pablo C. de, *Tepotzotlán: su historia y sus tesoros artisticos* (México: Porrúa, 1958).

Maza, Francisco de la, "El Colegio de Tepozotlán," *Cuadernos Médicos*, Vol. I (September, 1954), pp. 31–38.

Valle, Rafael Heliodoro, *El convento de Tepozotlán* (México: Talleres Gráficos del Museo Nacional, 1924).

Wuthenau, Alexander von, *Tepotzotlán, Arte y color en México: Kunst und farbe in Mexiko* (México: Von Stetten, 1940; English ed., 1941).

Zacatecas:

Maza, Francisco de la, "El arte en la ciudad de Nuestra Señora de los Zacatecas," *México en el Arte*, no. 7 (1949), pp. 5–16.

III. MINOR ARTS OF THE VICEREGAL ERA

Anderson, Lawrence Leslie, *The Art of the Silversmith in Mexico*, 2 vols. (New York: Oxford University, 1941).

Cervantes, Enrique A., *Herreros y forjadores poblanos* (México: Casas, 1933).

———, *Hierros de Oaxaca* (Oaxaca: Monografías del Gobierno del Estado, 1932).

———, *Loza blanca y azulejo de Puebla*, 2 vols. (México: 1939).

Cortés, Antonio, *Hierros forjados* (México: Museo Nacional de Arqueología, Historia, y Etnografía, 1935).

Romero de Terreros, Manuel, *Las artes industriales en la Nueva España* (México: P. Robredo, 1932).

Villegas, Victor Manuel, *Hierros coloniales en Zacatecas* (México: Imprenta Universitaria, 1955).

IV. PAINTING IN THE VICEREGAL ERA

Carrillo y Gariel, Abelardo, *Autógrafos . . . de pintores coloniales* (México: Imprenta Universitaria, 1953).

———, *Técnica de la pintura de Nueva España* (México: Imprenta Universitaria, 1946).

Romero Flores, Jesús, *Iconografía colonial; retratos de personajes notables en la historia colonial de México, existentes en el Museo Nacional* (México: Museo Nacional, 1940).

Soria, Martin, in George Kubler and Martin Soria, *Art and Architecture of Spain and Portugal and Their American Dominions: 1500–1800.* Especially pp. 305–316.

Toussaint, Manuel, *La pintura en México durante el siglo XVI* (México: Enciclopedia Ilustrada Mexicana, No. 2, 1936).

———, "La pintura mural en Nueva España," *Artes de México*, Vol. 4 (May–June, 1954), pp. 7–30.

———, *Pinturas murales en los conventos mexicanos del siglo XVI* (México: Ediciones de Arte, 1948).

Velázquez Chavez, Agustín, *Tres siglos de pintura colonial mexicana* (México: Polis, 1939).

V. SCULPTURE IN THE VICEREGAL PERIOD

Alt, Dr. (Gerardo Murillo), *Los Altares*, Vol. 5 of *Iglesias de México* (México: Secretaría de Hacienda, 1925).

Baird, Joseph A., Jr., "The Eighteenth Century Retable in the South of Spain, Portugal and México," Ph.D. thesis, Harvard University, 1951.

———, "Eighteenth Century Retables of the Bajío: The Querétaro Style," *Art Bulletin*, Vol. XXXV (September, 1953), pp. 195–216.

Carrillo y Gariel, Abelardo, *El cristo de Mexicaltzingo: tecnica de las esculturas en caña* (México: 1949).

Fernández, Justino, *El Retablo de los Reyes: estética del arte de la Nueva España* (México: Instituto de Investigaciones Estéticas, 1959).

Imaginería Colonial (México: Universidad . . . de México, 1941).

Maza, Francisco de la, *Arquitectura de los coros de monjas en México* (México: Imprenta Universitaria, 1956).

———, "Mexican Colonial Retables," *Gazette des Beaux-Arts*, Vol. XXV, series 6 (March, 1944).

———, *Las piras funerarias en la historia y en el arte de México* (México: Imprenta Universitaria, 1956).

———, *Retablos dorados de Nueva España* (México: Ediciones Mexicanas, 1950).

Soria, Martin, in George Kubler and Martin Soria, *Art and Architecture in Spain and Portugal and Their American Dominions: 1500–1800*. Especially pp. 165–169.

Weismann, Elizabeth Wilder, *Mexico in Sculpture* (Cambridge, Mass.: Harvard University Press, 1950); Spanish ed., with introduction in Spanish and text in English (México: Atlante, 1950).

Geography and History

SPAIN

Ballesteros y Beretta, D. Antonio, *Historia de España y su influencia en la historia universal*. 9 vols. (Barcelona: Salvat, 1918–1941).

Gams, Pius Bonifacius, *Die Kirchengeschichte von Spanien*, 3 vols. (Regensburg: G. J. Manz, 1879).

Sedgewick, Henry D., *Spain, A Short History of Its Politics, Literature and Art from Earliest Times to the Present*. Preface by J. D. M. Ford (Boston: Little, Brown, 1926).

SPANISH AMERICA

Alcázar Molina, Cayetano, *Los virreinatos en el siglo XVIII* (Barcelona: Salvat, 1945).

Wilgus, A. Curtis, *The Development of Hispanic America* (New York: Farrar, 1941).

———, *Histories and Historians of Hispanic America*, Series 1 and 2 (Washington, D. C.: Inter-American Bibliographical and Library Association Publications, 1936).

MEXICO

Bancroft, Hubert Howe, *History of Mexico*, 6 vols. (San Francisco: A. L. Bancroft & Co., 1883–1888).

Braden, Charles, *Religious Aspects of the Conquest of Mexico* (Durham, N. C.: Duke University Press, 1930).

Cuevas, Mariano, *Historia de la iglesia en México*. 5 vols., 2nd ed. (El Paso, Texas: Revista Catolica, 1928).

Gacetas de México. Intro. by González de Cossío to a selection of these papers, including all those published in 1722 and 1728–1731 (México: Secretaría de Educación Pública, 1949).

Handbook of Mexico (London: Intelligence Division, Naval Staff of Admiralty, 1928).

Hepburn, Andrew, *Complete Guide to Mexico* (New York: Doubleday, 1960).

Martin, Lawrence and Sylvia, *The Standard Guide to Mexico* (New York: Funk and Wagnalls, 1960).

Motolinía (Toríbio de Benavente), *History of the Indians of New Spain*, ed. by Elizabeth Andros Forster (Berkeley, Calif.: Cortes Society, 1950).

Parkes, Henry B., *A History of Mexico* (Boston: Houghton Mifflin, 1950).

Ricard, Robert, *La "Conquête Spirituelle" du Mexique* (Paris: Université de Paris, Travaux et Mémoires de l'Institut d'Ethnologie, No. 20, 1933); Spanish tr. by Angel Maria Garibay (México: Jus, 1947).

Riva Palacios, Vicente, *México a través de los siglos*, 5 vols. (México: Publicaciones Herrerias, 1939) (facsimile).

Simpson, Lesley B., *Many Mexicos*, 3rd ed. (Berkeley and Los Angeles: University of California Press, 1952).

Terry, T. Philip, *Terry's Guide to Mexico* (Hingham [Mass.], 1947).

CATALOGUE OF PLATES

The Catalogue of Plates is arranged alphabetically, to serve as an index. As in the plates themselves, there is a grouping of all features of a given building or complex of buildings—in this section, under the place or site name of the church. Each entry has a short recapitulation of historical facts relating to the foundation, construction, and embellishment of the building in question. This is followed by descriptive paragraphs for each plate in a grouping.

The alphabetizing is by place or site name, with the name of the state following in parenthesis, as Huejotzingo (Puebla). Certain cases present problems; the place or site (often no more than a crossroads) may be called by a combination of descriptive names—often a Christian saint's name and an Indian proper name or place designation. Thus, San Francisco Acatepec is listed under Acatepec. Where feasible, both the nature of the establishment (as "Monastery of") and its specific dedication are indicated; consistency here is difficult. Where no other qualification is indicated, the words "Church of" are usually implied before a proper name at any given site; thus, "Morelia (Michoacán), La Merced" means "Church of La Merced in Morelia (Michoacán)." Common usage in Mexico generally elects simply the place or site name of isolated, well-known buildings, particularly those of the sixteenth century, as sufficient identification; e.g., "Acolman" clearly means the monastery and church of the Augustinians at Acolman in the state of México. After the initial main entry in full, shortened forms are used wherever confusion with other buildings is unlikely. In certain place names, such as San Luis de Potosí, San Miguel de Allende, and San Cristóbal de Las Casas, the "de" is usually dropped in common usage. Again, the brief form is used after the first citation in full.

Some churches are identified by both their English and Spanish names. Almost all the hundreds of town and village parish churches in Mexico are referred to locally as "la parroquia," without any rigid consistency in adding the specific dedication of that church. Where a specific name is not commonly known or, indeed, ascertainable, the church is identified merely as "parish church (la parroquia)." A famous church with an established dedication, such as the parish church of Santa Prisca and San Sebastián in Taxco, is so indicated in the first citation; this church is then simply referred to as Santa Prisca. A pilgrimage church of the later seventeenth or eighteenth century in a relatively isolated place is identified as "pilgrimage church," with the specific local dedication in parentheses, as "La Cata (Guanajuato), Pilgrimage Church (El Santuario del Señor de Villaseca)." The well-known Santuario de la Soledad in Oaxaca is now clearly part of a large group of town churches.

Don and Fray when used as titles are capitalized here, as are La and El and their plurals. Although this is not common usage in Spanish, it more clearly identifies them as parts of proper names.

The orientation of Mexican churches between 1530 and 1810 was inconsistent and apparently governed by more than ecclesiastic necessity or tradition. It would be impossible to assume that the so-called "traditional" (essentially late medieval) placing of altar end at the east was observed with any consistency in Mexico. In a given town, individual churches may be oriented to each of the four points of the compass. Thus, in place of "north" and "south," "left" and "right" are generally used in this Catalogue. "Left" and "right" in this sense always refer to the spectator's left and right when he is facing the building or part being discussed.

SAN FRANCISCO ACATEPEC (Puebla)

San Francisco Acatepec

The construction of this church appears to have been initiated in the later seventeenth century; the fabric was essentially completed sometime in the eighteenth century, and the façade must date from 1750 or 1760. The interior suffered a devastating fire in late 1939, which destroyed much of the original polychromed plaster work. Some areas, especially that under the choir, fortunately were not touched, and suggest the splendor of the original decoration and its subtlety of color. Restoration has been under way since the fire.

SAN FRANCISCO ACATEPEC, CHURCH FAÇADE (pl. 104 and pl. 158, color)

This is one of the most extraordinary church fronts in all Mexico, and represents a culminating point of the Pueblan tile tradition. The façade proper, the tower, and *campanario*—and their supports—are covered with a variety of colored tile, blue, yellow, and white predominating in the façade proper. Late Baroque in its grouping of salient parts, its splayed sides, and its ascendant movement to a star-shaped window in the upper center, the façade has classicizing columns and half-columns in the first level and *estípite* pillars and pilasters in the second and third—dating it to the mid-eighteenth century. Numerous *Mudéjar* features (the beautifully paneled doors, the semblance of an *alfiz* enclosing a shell over the doors, the star window, and the strongly geometric character of the tile patterns) combine with a "pushed-up" cornice over the first and second level center to give this design vivacity and yet a remarkable clarity of parts. One of a group of tiled façades in the area—including Santa María Tonantzintla and San Bernardino Tlaxcalancingo—it is certainly the most dazzling of all.

SAN FRANCISCO ACATEPEC, DOOR TO BAPTISTRY (pl. 160, color)

The exuberant plaster foliation about the door combines the lushness of Late Baroque with a sharp contouring reminiscent of Mannerist strapwork. Curious heads interspersed in the writhing ornament are "provincial" in much the same manner as the Greco-Buddhist heads from Gandhara, and have an atavistic quality which could easily tempt one to see them as "Mexican Indian" rather than as gauchely charming expressions of local craftsmanship. Notable is the folk character of the doors themselves, with simplified *estípites* and angelic figures as vertical division bars. The mingling of authentic and exquisite colonial work with a casual and often mediocre modern taste in images or painting is typical of many modest Mexican churches; the result here is also partially colored by the notable eighteenth-century polychromed plaster, surviving the fire, on the underside of the *coro*—just above this door.

SAN FRANCISCO ACATEPEC, ST. FRANCIS AS PROTECTOR (RELIEF) (pl. 105)

San Francisco Acatepec is full of fragments of large ensembles, all disposed in a casual manner on provisional bases with touching if naïve garnishings of flowers. St. Francis (here with the stigmata and standing on the orb) protects a group of church dignitaries—pope, bishop, priest. The quality of carving and *estofado* is excellent, placing this group closer in spirit to the positive, lavishly robust character of the seventeenth century than to the eighteenth, with its rather effete elegance; however, it was probably executed early in the eighteenth century.

SAN FRANCISCO ACATEPEC, CHRIST AT THE COLUMN (SCULPTURE) (pl. 106)

Later colonial art continues the interest in particularly horrific images of Christ after his scourging. It is here, too, that a residual feeling in Mexican colonial art for the blood-bespattered images of the Aztec period continues to manifest itself. The incongruous neutrality of a large, white gown over this Christ spares twentieth-century sensibilities from the implications of torture. By contrast, the kneeling angel seems insipid—a perfect statement of the banality of much official ecclesiastical sculpture after 1720 or 1740.

SAN FRANCISCO ACATEPEC, THE DEAD CHRIST MOURNED AT THE FOOT OF THE CROSS (PAINTING) (pl. 107)

Inspired largely by Flemish sources of the later medieval period, a number of colonial Mexican paintings essentially bypassed or disregarded the developments of Baroque Italy and Spain. This painting, in the style of the Echaves (a family of important colonial Mexican painters), reflects a static, frontal composition popular just before 1500 in northern Europe. However, it is embued with the pathos of the sixteenth-century Spanish painter, Luis de Morales and probably dates from about 1750.

ACOLMAN (México)

AUGUSTINIAN MONASTERY OF SAN AGUSTÍN

The community of Acolman was ceded after the Conquest to Pedro de Solís and his son Francisco. A group of Augustinian friars under Jorge de Ávila took over the religious direction of the area in 1539, following a Franciscan foundation that had come from San Juan Teotihuacán. Twenty-four friars were in residence by 1580. The present monastic complex appears to date largely after 1550; an interior capital is dated 1558, and the façade 1560. An inscription on the arch of the *coro* refers to a reconstruction of 1735, when the vault was modified and interior pilasters and exterior buttresses were added. During the colonial period, in attempts to control the rivers of this area, a dam was constructed which wreaked havoc on the church and cloisters. The monastery was submerged to a depth of over six feet, and a thick layer of silt covered the church floor and virtually inundated the cloisters. Restoration has continued since 1920, once again exposing the church façade in its entirety and cleaning all interior parts of debris—with the result that the atrium is terraced down to the old level of construction; damage to the stone carving of the façade measures the level of inundation. Especially notable at Acolman is the *tequitqui* stone cross in a separate enclosure before the atrium (today with a road between). Eight feet high, it is a particularly powerful expression of Indian conventions in the early viceregal period. (See Wilder Weismann, *Mexico in Sculpture*, p. 7, for a photograph.) It seems to be earlier than the architectural sculpture here, but after the Franciscan occupancy. The grim-faced virgin (a colonial variant of the Aztec mother goddess, Coatlicue) at the base of the cross is probably later than the cross itself.

ACOLMAN, GENERAL VIEW OF AUGUSTINIAN CHURCH AND
      MONASTERY (pl. 156, color)

The battlemented silhouette of the church, with its simple *companario* above the façade, the sturdy arches of the *portería* to the right of the church (possibly a *capilla de indios?*), and the rich Plateresque ornamentation of the church façade proper, mark San Agustín at Acolman as a classic sixteenth-century structure. McAndrew has indicated that

these were not essentially "fortress-monasteries," despite their heavy, pseudo-fortified character; nevertheless, psychologically they dominate the countryside around them, much as a medieval castle did in Europe. The rubble stone construction of the walls has been plastered over; the carefully fitted stones of the façade proper lent themselves to fine carving. The church is about 205 feet long, 56 feet wide, and 70 feet high. There are two cloisters with monastic cells, and the usual service quarters.

ACOLMAN, FAÇADE OF AUGUSTINIAN CHURCH (pl. 28)

An inscription on the rose-tan stone façade reads as follows in translation: "This work was finished in the year 1560, during the reign of the king Don Felipe our Lord, son of the Emperor Carlos V, and governing this New Spain his illustrious (the second) Viceroy, Don Luis de Velasco, with whose favor it was built." A Spanish master probably carved the façade; its source is possibly the Colegiata de Santa María at Calatayud, Spain. Typically Plateresque is the combination of parts here: a door with double Renaissance archivolts above, decorated with fruit; classical composite columns with Plateresque sections below and ribbon garniture; St. Paul under a deep, Gothic-inspired canopy, with a Renaissance angel below; seahorses in the main frieze above the door, and the Mudéjar paneling of the door itself.

ACOLMAN, CHURCH INTERIOR TOWARD *retablo mayor*
      (pl. 29)

The construction of the presbytery, with its elaborate late medieval ribbed vault, dates from 1558. Important frescoes, black, white, and orange—representing church dignitaries and saints seated on thrones, as well as a coat of arms and inscriptions—cover the walls of the presbytery. The *retablo mayor* is a work of about 1690, and was put here in the twentieth century to replace the original *retablo mayor*. Other retables, with *salomónicas* and *estípites*, as well as painted retables of the eighteenth century, are ranged along the side walls.

ACOLMAN, FIRST CLOISTER (pl. 30)

This first small cloister at Acolman may date from the Franciscan occupancy, or it may be part of an early Augustinian church. Flattened arches on piers with a barrel-vaulted corridor on the ground level and a wooden roofed second level suggest the simple constructive techniques in rubble masonry of the first periods of Christian building in Mexico. Primitive fresco paintings decorate the walls. The stone cross is similar in its stark simplicity to that in the atrium of the Franciscan establishment at Cuernavaca.

ACOLMAN, SECOND CLOISTER (pl. 31)

The more sophisticated proportional relationship of arches in the first and second levels of the second or large cloister at Acolman (in units of triple arches over doubled arches), the more refined construction of fitted stone, and the bold if curiously abstract carvings of capitals and bases of the columns indicate a marked development of both technical control and idea in this work, which dates about twenty years after the first cloister. Both levels of this cloister are unvaulted.

ACOLMAN, DOOR IN SECOND LEVEL OF SECOND CLOISTER (pl. 32)

Linen-fold paneling on the door in the late medieval manner combines with a simplified Renaissance foliated pattern on the painted pilasters and arch above. A section of the quotations which encircle this level of the cloister appears in the frescoed frieze under the wooden beamed ceiling.

ACOLMAN, WALL, CRUCIFIXION (FRESCO), SECOND LEVEL OF SECOND CLOISTER (pl. 33)

Inspired by a variety of European sources of the fifteenth and sixteenth century (German prints, Italian and German ornamental panels) this powerful fresco in black and white reflects the continuing importance of the graphic arts as models for Mexican decoration and painting. The sun and moon motifs will echo down through the entire viceregal period— a fortuitous association of old European astrological and religious symbols with the importance given these same symbols in Indian art. Most of the painting at Acolman has been brought to light after painstaking removal of surface plaster and paint added at later periods.

ACTOPAN (Hidalgo)

AUGUSTINIAN MONASTERY OF SAN NICOLÁS

The large and elaborate monastic complex of the Augustinians at Actopan is one of the most impressive centers of sixteenth-century architecture and painting in the New World. The beginning of construction on the present buildings is variously dated from 1546 or about 1550 (Actopan was made a priorate in 1548). The work was under the direction of Fray Andrés de Mata and continued under Fray Martín de Acebeido. The features of a great Augustinian *convento* are developed here with individual variations—a commanding vaulted church in stone, with battlemented top and tower, and a refined façade; the massive quasi-Romanesque, quasi-Renaissance *portería;* the cloister with pointed Gothic arches below and rounded arches above; the spacious stair hall with frescoed walls; the coffered refectory; the open chapel, here adjacent to the rear of the church. Patrons of the construction were the two leading local Indians, Don Juan Inica Actopan and Don Pedro Izcuicuitlapilco.

ACTOPAN, FAÇADE OF AUGUSTINIAN CHURCH (pl. 24)

Fray Andrés de Mata, the first director of construction at Actopan, lived in Italy for some time before his vocation in Mexico. The basic design of this façade is Plateresque in its simple framing of door with columns and arch, and its small window with flanking Plateresque columns above. However, the relatively pure classicism of columns on the lower part of the façade (drawn out especially on the sides in Mannerist elongation) and the use of a perspective coffered vault above the door suggest a definite knowledge of Italian Renaissance architecture. Most of the ornamental motifs are Renaissance (the angelic children's heads in panels of the door arch, and so on). The extremely tall, empty niches between the half-columns are more Mannerist, making this a progressive design for its period. Towers of the size seen here are most common on Augustinian monasteries after 1550; Kubler relates the particular form of the Actopan tower to secular sources in Spain.

ACTOPAN, CHURCH BATTLEMENTS (pl. 25)

Battlements and mock sentry boxes on the upper part of the church at Actopan are bristlingly defensive in appearance. They appear to have been largely decorative in most of these monastic churches, with a few exceptions in western Mexico. Although the Indian populace had ample provocation (from rapacious secular administrators) to revolt or riot, there are virtually no instances of attack on the *conventos*.

ACTOPAN, FRESCOED STAIR HALL (pl. 26)

The very large squared, open staircase (a type first used in Spain early in the sixteenth century) in the monastery at Actopan is decorated with paintings of various church dignitaries and historical-devotional scenes. The composition of the individual sections relating to the saints and other church dignitaries is derived from northern European painting and prints, although the framing of the ensemble in pseudo architecture implies Italian and Spanish sources— Italian for the abundant decorative friezes with urns, *rinceaux*, and real or fantastic creatures.

ACTOPAN, REFECTORY (pl. 27)

Actual and painted coffered ceilings are often found in the cloister vaults of Dominican monasteries of the sixteenth century. The superb rose-colored and flower-patterned enrichment of the octagonal coffers in this Augustinian refectory, as well as the illusionistic hexagonal painted coffers between, is both extensive and impressive, reiterating the influence of Italy on Fray Andrés de Mata. (Angulo suggests the use of the treatise of the Italian architect, Sebestiano Serlio, in a Spanish translation of 1563, as a model for the coffering, which also occurs in a related form in the open chapel at Actopan.) However, the great tunnel- or barrel-vaulted refectory implies structurally the massive, simple construction of an earlier Romanesque era.

CALPAN (Puebla)

FRANCISCAN MONASTERY OF SAN ANDRÉS

Calpan was served by the Franciscans after 1525. The present monastic ensemble dates from about 1548; the work was directed by Fray Juan de Alameda, the builder of the Franciscan houses at Huejotzingo and Huaquechula. Aside from the elegant, tall façade of the church, the most important elements at Calpan are the extraordinary *capillas posas*, related in style and period to those at Huejotzingo. Constructed near the base of Mt. Popocatepetl,

Calpan lies at the end of a tortuous road, branching off the Mexico-Puebla highway at Huejotzingo. Its relative difficulty of access makes the sixteenth-century work at Calpan all the more astonishing when seen.

CALPAN, FAÇADE OF FRANCISCAN CHURCH (pl. 8)

As many writers have remarked, the total effect of the tall, slender façade of San Andrés at Calpan is Gothic. Despite the presence of a typical late medieval window with two arches and thin colonnette between, in the upper center of this design, and the essentially non-Classical quality of capitals and central sections of the incised half-columns flanking the angels above the door, some of the individual motifs, such as the shell at the top, reveal Renaissance influence. Virtually unique as ornamental forms are the tall maguey flowers crowning the half-columns at either side, as much like torches from a procession as they are like natural forms. The Franciscan cord is used in the manner of an *alfiz* around the double window, recalling the use of the cord at Huejotzingo. Numerous representations of the stigmata and other Franciscan insignia spot the surface of the façade; and a relief of St. Andrew, tutelary protector of this monastery, occupies the center. Angulo astutely suggests that this façade, related to the late medieval work of northern Spain, is also almost a forecast of the later nineteenth century.

CALPAN, SOUTH SIDE OF NORTHEAST *posa* (pl. 9)

The four *posas* at Calpan are especially richly decorated. That at the northeast has three rather than the usual two sides carved with motifs and symbols, because it stands by the northern gate. The subjects of each face are: the Virgin of the Seven Sorrows (or the Seven Gifts of the Holy Spirit) on the east side; the Assumption of the Virgin on the south side; the Annunciation on the west side. Obviously of Indian workmanship, the carving of these *posas* is nevertheless boldly Christian in conception and vigorous in execution. Each *posa* has a different top, and the moldings and ornamental crestings are remarkably varied. Roughly constructed walls of more recent times now fill in the original arched openings of this particular *posa*. (The processional order of the *posas* would appear to begin at the right as a person emerged from the church door [that is, at the northeast *posa*] and continue counterclockwise around the atrium.)

CALPAN, WEST SIDE OF NORTHEAST *posa* (pl. 10)

The Annunciation on this face of the northeast *posa* verges on unintentional parody in the athletic springiness of the angel and the voluminous resilience of the Virgin. The lilies and the dove seem caught in a passing rain—actually rays of light. The unconcerned spotting of compositional parts is accentuated by isolated medallions of the stigmata and the symbolic crossed arms of Christ and St. Francis, repeated in the frieze and corner pilasters below in more floreate form.

CALPAN, NORTHWEST *posa* (pl. 11)

The south side of this *posa* (brilliantly lighted in the photograph) has an angel with a Franciscan shield, flanked by symbolic medallions; the darker east side is carved with angels and instruments of the Passion. Especially interesting is the domed top and the now broken cresting of the *posa* walls—related to the so-called Manueline qualities of the side door (or Puerta de la Porciúncula) of the Franciscan church at Huejotzingo.

CALPAN, EAST SIDE OF SOUTHWEST *posa* (pl. 12)

As George Kubler and Elizabeth Wilder Weismann have demonstrated, this Last Judgment was derived from a woodcut in the *Flos Sanctorum* of Fray Pedro de la Vega, a work first printed in Zaragoza, Spain, in 1521. A prototype of the woodcut appeared in various late fifteenth-century books. The seated Savior with a lily and a sword above his head, the Virgin and St. John as intercessors, the trumpeting angels, and the souls rising from their tombs—all appear in the European original. Yet the effect is infinitely more powerful than the tepid print might imply. On the north side of this *posa* are archangels, one labeled San Miguel.

CALPAN, DETAIL OF EAST SIDE OF SOUTHWEST *posa* (pl. 13)

Christ as the Savior here could possibly be interpreted as the great pre-Conquest divinity, Quetzalcóatl, in his muscular power of body and gesture.

The trumpeting angel on the right has an Indianized face. Yet as in much of the so-called Indian influence on early Conquest art, there is comparatively little specific use of pre-Conquest forms. It is the flattened and yet bold carving technique and the preoccupation with symmetrically disposed elements on a neutral surface that recall the manner of pre-Conquest sculptors. Still, this flattening is also common to carving in "colonial" areas of all times.

CALPAN, WEST SIDE OF SOUTHEAST *posa* (pl. 14)

This face of the southeast *posa* has a St. John the Evangelist in the niche, framed by four medallions with symbols of the Evangelists. The broken and yet almost continuous vertical moldings recall the façade of the church at Calpan with its tall, thin lines of movement unresolved at the top of each side. Surprisingly, if the pyramidal roof is excepted, the general design of this face reminds one of the curious ancient Roman monument of the baker Eurysaces, now outside the Porta Maggiore. On the north side of the *posa* is a carving of God the Father as Pantocrator.

CALPAN, DETAIL OF WEST SIDE OF SOUTHEAST *posa* (pl. 15)

Here again is proof positive of the almost complete dominance of European sources in these sixteenth-century ornamental carvings. The trumpeting angel with *rinceaux* and roses in the frieze, the foliation and IHS letters of the pilasters, and the acanthus leaves and ox skulls of the base are wholly Roman or Renaissance Italian. The sharp edges of these flat bands of ornament, suggesting something stamped from clay rather than carved, represent a simplification and stereotyping of sophisticated sources which could have been done in Armenia or Palmyra as well as in Mexico. The end result, however, is not to be dismissed as provincial in a weak or diluted sense. It is as vigorous and beautiful as the similar work of Romanesque France.

CHOLULA (Puebla)

Cholula has long been fabled to have many churches. The myth that it had one for each day of the year was apparently started through a misunderstanding of one of Cortés' letters, in which he referred to the many towers (pyramids?) of pre-Conquest Cholula. According to de la Maza, there are about thirty-nine churches of various sizes in this immediate area, including an important Franciscan monastic church and dependencies, and the dramatically situated pilgrimage shrine of Nuestra Señora de los Remedios on top of the largest pre-Conquest teocalli in Mexico.

CHOLULA, GENERAL VIEW OF PYRAMID AND CHURCH OF NUESTRA SEÑORA DE LOS REMEDIOS (pl. 101)

As in much post-Conquest religious siting, an attempt was made to combine the sanctity of an Indian area of veneration with a Christian foundation. The gigantic, somewhat irregular teocalli at Cholula (about 1000 feet on a side and 200 feet high) early had a Catholic church replacing the Indian temple on its top. The present church dates from the eighteenth and nineteenth century (it was rebuilt after an earthquake of 1864 and reconsecrated on August 24, 1874); it is undistinguished except for its effective silhouette of high tiled dome and twin towers and rich, if coarse, "Republican Baroque" interior. Occupying a plateau on top of the pyramid—now an overgrown hill—the church has a rather casually planned stair of access 14 feet wide, instead of the elaborate terraced and divided staircases of the great Portuguese and Brazilian pilgrimage churches.

The view shown includes a small church near the Mexico City–Puebla highway where it branches off to Cholula.

CUERNAVACA (Morelos)

FRANCISCAN MONASTERY OF LA ANUNCIACIÓN DE NUESTRA SEÑORA (NOW CATHEDRAL)

The Franciscans were established at Cuernavaca by 1526; the formal foundation of a monastic house for the Friars Minor was ratified in 1529. Construction on the church was spread over much of the sixteenth century, ending in its main elements about 1574 (this also included lengthening the building to the east). The design is attributed to Francisco Becerra, a Spanish architect who eventually went to Peru. The side portal on the north is dated 1552, while the upper part of the façade tower is dated 1713. In addition to the church with its modernized interior

(and its interesting colonial frescoes, now being uncovered), the complex at Cuernavaca includes an important open chapel and a handsome church of the Third Order of Franciscans, principally of the eighteenth century. The crenelated atrium has agreeable planting of the type that accords with Cuernavaca's celebrated mild climate; indeed, the Franciscan house here seems to have been especially used by the aged and infirm members of the order. The church is now a cathedral.

CUERNAVACA, GENERAL VIEW OF CATHEDRAL AND OPEN CHAPEL FROM NORTH SIDE OF ATRIUM (pl. 18)

Standing before the side portal of the Third Order church, one can include in his range of vision some of the most important elements of the Franciscan establishment at Cuernavaca—the church with its simple battlemented top, the staged tower, the open chapel, and the atrium cross. Beyond the photograph, to the left, is the important north portal of the church and that comparatively rare form in Mexico, a flying buttress, used to support the church walls and vault and similar to the perforated pier buttresses of the open chapel.

CUERNAVACA, OPEN CHAPEL OF CATHEDRAL (pl. 19)

Kubler implies that it was unlikely that this structure was ever used for celebration of the Mass in the sixteenth century, and that it should therefore be considered a *capilla de indios* rather than a *capilla abierta*. It faces north, rather than west, which was the usual orientation for sixteenth-century open chapels. During the sixteenth and seventeenth centuries it appears to have been used as a *portería* or gathering place for Indian groups. Its present revision with an altar on a stepped platform is due to von Wuthenau's restoration of the structure in the twentieth century. Though the chapel is explicitly Gothic in its battlements and buttresses as well as its partial rib vaulting, it has a Romanesque solidity in its wide entrance arches and massive supporting piers.

CUERNAVACA, ATRIUM CROSS OF CATHEDRAL (pl. 20)

A simple cross of the sixteenth century was re-erected in its present location in the twentieth century after having been moved in the intervening period. It is mounted on a stepped platform of rubble masonry with corner merlons. This appropriately symbolizes the importance of the stepped pyramid in pre-Conquest times and the military character of the early post-Conquest era, with the entire combination dominated spiritually by the cross. At the foot of the cross there is a depression in the stone platform, which Wilder Weismann believes to represent a *cuauxicalli,* or Aztec ceremonial receptacle for the blood of sacrificial victims—here appropriated to the Christian Passion. The stone skull atop the cross has several implications: the importance of exposed skulls in pre-Conquest Indian ceremonials, its importance to devotional representation of St. Francis, and its overtones of Golgotha (the Place of the Skull), the site of the Crucifixion.

CUERNAVACA, SIDE PORTAL OF CATHEDRAL (pl. 21)

An arresting combination of ornamental and symbolic forms are present around the north portal of the Franciscan monastic church at Cuernavaca. Half-columns—more Romanesque than Renaissance—frame a well-proportioned arched door. Above, a steep pediment encloses a medallion and a niche with a grim pile of bones inside and angelic figure reliefs at either side. A tall, rectilinear frame in the manner of an *alfiz* caps the design and encloses a cross with skull and crossbones at its foot. Dated 1552 by an inscription, this door continues the morbid implications of the atrium cross, drawing in part on pre-Conquest elements of sacrifice and bone exposure, in part on Christian and Franciscan preoccupations with death and penitence. Especially for the sixteenth century with its *Ars Moriendi,* or manuals of dying, this fascination with physical death is understandable.

CUERNAVACA, STAGED TOWER OF CATHEDRAL (pl. 22)

From an inscription cut in an angle of the base, it is apparent that most of this lofty bell tower was built about 1713. The staged tower is, of course, a characteristic eighteenth-century building form, usually appearing in the pattern of twin staged towers flanking a church façade. Towers on sixteenth-century Franciscan churches are rare; but this one accords as well with its simple church fabric as the elaborate north façade tower at Chartres, France, does with its ear-

lier parts. The distinctly local variant of Corinthian pilasters on each stage are covered with cut-out ornament that combines Mudéjar formality with the *élan* of strapwork.

CUILAPAN (Oaxaca)

DOMINICAN MONASTERY OF SANTIAGO

The Dominicans were established at this southerly site by 1555. Three men are particularly associated with the buildings: Domingo de Aguiñaga, a friend of Ignatius Loyola; the Galician friar, Agustín de Salazar; and a Portuguese lay brother, Antonio Barbosa. Fray Agustín de Salazar arrived in 1559 and remained prior for twenty-six years; he was universally admired by the natives, and in 1581 wrote his *Relación de Cuilapan.* During his priorate, Antonio Barbosa designed the first church (finished 1568), which is of a type rare in Mexico of the period. Built with a nave and two aisles, it had a noble nave arcade and wooden roof in the Italian manner, although the immediate inspiration came from similar wooden roofed buildings in the Iberian area. A second church with a single nave was discontinued in the 1570's, by order of the *audiencia,* or colonial high court.

CUILAPAN, GENERAL VIEW OF TWO DOMINICAN CHURCHES (pl. 64)

The three-aisled plan of the first church and its extremely sober classicist character link this building to a small group of purist churches of the later sixteenth century, including Tecali and Zacatlán. Although all are generally related—with smallish façade towers or tower bases, an essentially Renaissance inspired façade with triangular or semicircular pediment above—Cuilapan is altogether heavier and lower than the others, reflecting its construction in earthquake territory. Furthermore, its interior elevation, with a clerestory under a gabled timber roof, is closer to Santo Domingo in Chiapa de Corzo. Both the serene first church and the unfinished second church at Cuilapan are in ruins.

CUILAPAN, INTERIOR OF EARLIER CHURCH (pl. 65)

Because of the certainty of severe earthquakes in southern Mexico, especially in the Oaxaca area, the

88 *Catalogue of Plates*

Dominicans built their churches with resistant stone walls that were low and heavy. Thus the arches of the façade, the nave arcade, and the side doors are rather more Romanesque than Renaissance. Ricard was led to believe that the numerous side doors gave the aisles inside the form of open chapels, related to the church nave. Kubler prefers to think that the extreme length of the church in relation to its present width, and the width of the nave in relation to the narrow aisles, indicates that a five-aisled church was intended, or more likely that the doors of the aisles— now opening to the outside—were intended to open into rows of chapels (which might have been built of perishable materials).

CUILAPAN, CHOIR AREA OF SECOND CHURCH (pl. 66)

The second monastic church at Cuilapan, which was discontinued during the 1570's, still retains the enormous supports for the vault under the *coro* at the entrance to the church. They are, in a sense, sections of massive piers or columns, treated here like corbels, from the top of which spring the fragments of vaulting still preserved. Higher on the wall are slightly smaller repetitions of these same corbels for the vault above the choir. The whole subject of late medieval vaulting has recently been reconsidered, after the researches of nineteenth- and early twentieth-century students of this science were found to contain somewhat exaggerated claims for the importance of the ribs as a structural foundation for Gothic vaulting. Here, as in much of sixteenth-century Mexican ribbed vaulting, the main ribs and tiercerons are an integral part of the whole vault surface—essentially carved enrichments of that surface. The ogival arch of the door under the *coro* is an excellent example of the rather casual attitude of the masons during this period to the relation of fitted and rubble construction; the voussoirs of the arch end in jagged contours above, though their underside is carved in the elegant ogival curve.

CUITZEO (Michoacan)

AUGUSTINIAN MONASTERY OF SANTA MARÍA MAGDALENA

The earliest converts at this site were made by the Franciscan, Fray Juan de San Miguel. In 1550 the area was assigned to the Augustinians, and on November 1 of that year the cornerstone of the present church was laid. The plan of the church is essentially that of the Augustinian monastic church at Yuririapundaro, not far to the east, except that at Cuitzeo the comparatively unusual transept of Yuriria was omitted. The design may have been by Pedro del Toro. Among the resident friars were Miguel de Alvarado, related to Diego de Chávez (active at Yuriria) and Francisco de Villafuerte, who is thought to be responsible for undertaking the construction of the beautiful façade. Work was especially active here in the 1590's (under Fray Gerónimo de Morante) and continued into the seventeenth century; the tower base with an *espadaña* is by Fray Gerónimo de Magdalena (1612). Interesting frescoes by Fray Matías Palacios were also executed in the seventeenth century.

CUITZEO, GENERAL VIEW OF AUGUSTINIAN CHURCH (pl. 38)

In addition to the superb façade of the church at Cuitzeo, signed by a native craftsman, Francisco Juan Metl, there is the tower and *espadaña* to the left and the *portería* to the right, with a crenelated top. Cuitzeo, with its lake setting, is now on a good road from Morelia to Salamanca; along with nearby Yuririapundaro, it is one of the most attractive of the Augustinian establishments in this former frontier area of western Mexico.

CUITZEO, *espadaña* (pl. 39)

In general the bells of these sixteenth-century Augustinian monastery churches were either in a rather modest wall belfry (*espadaña*) above the façade, as at Acolman, or in a true tower, as at Actopan, which latter could be more accurately called a *campanario*. At Cuitzeo there is a sturdy tower base, but at the upper level of the façade a more monumental *espadaña* with three arched openings faces the atrium and lake.

GUADALAJARA (Jalisco)

SANTA MONICA

Founded under the dedication of Incarnation of the Indies, a convent was initiated here about 1700. The present church for Augustinian nuns was begun about 1720 and finished *ca.* 1730 or 1733 (some authorities say 1722 or as late as 1740).

GUADALAJARA, ONE OF THE PAIRED FAÇADES OF SANTA MONICA (pl. 130)

Nuns' churches were particularly a phenomenon of the eighteenth century in Mexico, as they were in Venice. In Mexico, the long narrow interior was usually entered through a pair of façades on the flank of the church—approximately alike—which provided access for local parishioners. The nuns (not numerous for any one building) were accommodated in a smaller section at the back of the church, divided from the worldly worshipers by a thick, but essentially ornamental, wrought iron grill (that is, one could see through it). Thus, in most such churches the nuns occupied part of a choir (*coro alto*) and an under choir (*coro bajo*) behind the grill. The façades at Santa Monica are splendid examples of the *salomónica* fashion, beginning to wane in the 1730's. In addition to the lush foliation of the helicoid three-quarter and half-columns, there are extraordinary angelic caryatid pilasters between the columns of the first level. The crisp patterning of the lower sections of the upper columns—reminiscent of strapwork—and the imaginative if rather unclassical ornamentation of entablatures in both levels of the façade are conceptually superior to academic work of the same era. These gray-yellow façades prepare one for the more inclusive fantasy of the *parroquia* of Zacatecas (now a cathedral) (pl. 132).

GUADALAJARA, SAN CRISTÓBAL (SCULPTURE) AT CORNER OF SANTA MONICA (pl. 131)

Authorities differ in dating this powerful if awkward figure in a corner niche on the exterior of Santa Monica. Toussaint inclined to a date in the seventeenth century. It seems, however, that Wilder Weismann's suggestion of the eighteenth century is more correct for this deliberately archaizing work, so closely related in form and idea to the folk character of the angels in high relief or the angelic caryatid pilasters of the façades here. Wilder Weismann further suggests that the hole in the Christ Child's breast is based on the practice of placing an obsidian disk in the same relative position in pre-Conquest figures.

GUANAJUATO (Guanajuato)

FORMER JESUIT CHURCH OR LA COMPAÑÍA (NOW CHURCH OF SAN FELIPE NERI)

The Jesuits arrived in Guanajuato in 1732. Early housed in private dwellings, they received a formal foundation here in 1744, and began their large church on August 6, 1747. The plan was provided by the Bethlehemite monk, Fray José de la Cruz; the later phases of construction (to the dedication date of November 8, 1765) were under Felipe Ureña. A number of distinguished rectors succeeded each other in the eighteenth century, including the Guanajuato-born Jesuit, José Joaquín de Sardaneta y Legaspi, brother of the wealthy Marqués de San Juan de Rayas in Guanajuato. After the expulsion of the Jesuits from Hispanic dominions in 1767, the buildings languished until they were taken over by the Filippine fathers (Oratorians) in 1785. The Neo-Classical dome collapsed in 1808, and the present dome was rebuilt in 1869–1884, when the church interior was also remodeled.

The Jesuit foundation in Guanajuato included a school, which later became the Filippine college, the Colegio del Estado, and finally (in 1945) the University of Guanajuato.

GUANAJUATO, DOME OF SAN FELIPE NERI FROM PATIO OF THE UNIVERSITY (pl. 147)

The beautiful roseate stone of the Guanajuato area (there are other colors available as well) is particularly well matched and cut in the construction of the patio, with its Neo-Classical, or rather Neo-Renaissance, arcades. The dome with coupled columns and its drums diminishing in radius still suggests the Late Baroque in form; however, the purist ornament and the tall, oval windows recall French classicism. On one side of this patio adjacent to the former church of La Compañia is a modern staircase with two fine late eighteenth-century church portals from nearby Marfil, used here as doorways to the interior of one of the University buildings.

SAN ROQUE

Virtually nothing has been written about this church, with its very restrained façade and Mudéjar-inspired doors. It must date from the eighteenth century in its present form.

GUANAJUATO, FAÇADE OF SAN ROQUE (pl. 148)

The plain classicist façade of San Roque is one of many examples of continued fondness for a rather dry, academic façade type, related in a modest way to the churches of later sixteenth-century Rome, and showing the use of "shadow-pilasters" (a wider wall pilaster behind a less wide pilaster—the whole moving forward in depth through a broken entablature). A small plaza in the foreground is used during the summer months for the production of old Spanish plays. The bent lamps, probably twentieth century, have simply never been straightened after accidental twisting.

HUEJOTZINGO (Puebla)

FRANCISCAN MONASTERY OF THE ARCHANGEL SAN MIGUEL

The territory where the great Franciscan monastery of Huejotzingo was erected had been the land of an Indian group closely allied to the *conquistadores*. It had been given after the Conquest to Diego de Ordáz and later to the Crown. The site for the monastery was chosen between 1524 and 1529, and a first church was begun after 1529 (to 1539), of which there are no remains today. This first church may have been overseen by the energetic Franciscan, Fray Juan de Alameda. Kubler thinks that first church may have been a large, three-aisled building. The present church was begun about 1544 and probably completed by 1571.

HUEJOTZINGO, ATRIUM AND FAÇADE OF FRANCISCAN CHURCH (pl. 1)

The muscular vigor of the cross in the foreground (apparently taken from the top of one of the *posas*, or very closely related to them) is an obvious survival of the vigor of Aztec sculpture as well as an indication of Indian preoccupations with themes of penitence and death. The crown of thorns is very close in form to two Aztec serpents intertwined. In the background the superb façade of San Miguel at Huejotzingo reveals the canted, corner pier buttresses seen on San Gabriel at Cholula and elsewhere; but the

decoration of the façade is unique in Mexico. Generally of extreme and elegant simplicity, it has a masterful organization of Gothic and Renaissance elements around the door and window in the center. The crenelation above is more obviously decorative than on Augustinian monastic churches (see Actopan, pl. 25); to the lower right, one arch of the massive *portería* appears. The color (in pinkish stone with a brown surround) is as restrained as the design.

HUEJOTZINGO, LOWER CENTER OF CHURCH FAÇADE (pl. 2)

The sinuous profile of the arch over the door is essentially Late Gothic, although there are Islamic undertones here as well. Unusual is the carrying up of the colonnettes at each side of the door into the arch area as a frame, or what might be called a more playful, Gothicizing *alfiz*. The deeply splayed arch is firmly and yet expansively founded on the repeated horizontal moldings which run out from the door colonnette capitals to the tall, pseudo-classicist colonnettes at the extreme left and right of the portal area. Above the arch, under a beautifully disposed rectilinear frame of the Franciscan cord, are seven medallions with the names of Jesus and Christ. Exquisite refinements of idea suggest a great master: the closely spaced repetition of the pearls of Castile on one of the horizontal moldings under the side of the doorway arch, and the incised disks at the lower left and right of the façade, echoing the circles of the medallions above; the slight suggestion of movement in the stubby, twisted bases of the door colonnettes, reinforcing and anticipating the outward thrust of the splayed arch above. The leaves of a wooden door give subtle reinforcement to the strong vertical and horizontal lines in the stone design around them through rows of nails with heads in the form of flowerets. The holy water basins or stoups at lower left and right are of the eighteenth century.

HUEZOTZINGO, *portería* OF MONASTERY (pl. 3)

The designer again displays his mastery of a wide variety of stylistic backgrounds in this monumental *portería*. Of a Romanesque heaviness in proportion (especially in the great central pier or column), the arches will remind American readers of Henry Hobson Richardson's enthusiasm for the low, wide entrance arch. Decorative motifs include the pearls of Castile, the thick chain (seen on a *posa*), a plaited cord, foliation, and stylized flower patterns that look like the cross of Alcántara used by the Dominicans (over the arch at the right). Again the *alfiz* appears, here as a simple rectilinear molding around the arches. The remarkable sophistication of sources is expressed in a formality that balances between European professionalism and local vividness of idea and expression.

HUEZOTZINGO, NORTHEAST *posa* (pl. 4)

One of the *posas* at Huejotzingo is dated 1550. All are more uniform in structure and decoration than those at Calpan, not far away. These curious little processional oratories are ornamented with flying angels, framed by a bold Franciscan cord in the shape of an *alfiz*, as well as with other Franciscan insignia. Angulo has drawn an interesting parallel between the four flattened insignia above the *alfiz* and the circles in the same relative space on pre-Conquest Aztec temples. The cresting survives in part elsewhere in the town of Huejotzingo. Interiorly, the *posas* have false vaults and some remnants of painted decoration. Somewhat more isolated today by the growth of vegetation in the atrium (which is exceptionally large in dimension), the *posas* are outposts of religious enthusiasm that remind one of the adaptability of the friars to the need for pageantry among their converts.

HUEJOTZINGO, DETAIL OF NORTHEAST *posa* (pl. 5)

Winged figures in the spandrels of an arch, seen in both Rome and Sassanian Persia of the later antique period, are here given a more explicitly Christian importance since they bear the instruments of the Passion. The flat cut-out character of certain related monuments (Tepoztlán and Huaquechula) is less obvious at Huejotzingo and Calpan, where the carving has a plasticity which is at once European and Aztec. The heavy plaited and knotted cord has suggested a Portuguese background of the master craftsman to some writers, since it has the pseudo-marine rope quality of Manueline ornament in Portugal, seen also in the Puerta de la Porciúncula at Huejotzingo (the side portal of the church).

HUEJOTZINGO, NAVE VAULTS OF CHURCH (pl. 6)

Some Franciscan churches were not entirely covered over with rib vaulting, not because the builders lacked enthusiasm for this late Gothic roof type but because some Franciscan churches—among the earliest in construction in Mexico—had to rely on less skilled, or perhaps less well trained, craftsmen. At Huejotzingo, however, the rib system is particularly handsome, with its curved and straight patterned interlaces of main ribs, tiercerons, and liernes. Three distinctly different patterns are used in the four bays of the church proper (the two central bays are alike), and another variation covers the presbytery. As stated in the section on Cuilapan in this Catalogue, the whole problem of late medieval vaulting is undergoing more careful study at the present time. The once strongly emphasized theory of skeleton and panel construction with ribs and stone fill tends now to be less obvious. Many of the vaults were independent of their ribs; the latter were, then, ornamental patterns on the surface. The painting of this interior dates from the nineteenth century.

HUEJOTZINGO, *retablo mayor* OF CHURCH (pl. 7)

The great *retablo mayor* of Huejotzingo is signed and dated, although the inscription does not permit a conclusive proof of the date. It has been variously read as 1570, 1580, or 1586. Kubler inclines to the first date, relating the retable to the later phases of construction on the church. Wilder Weismann prefers the date of 1580, as the painter who signed these parts of the whole, Simón Pereyns, was working on a retable for the old cathedral of Mexico City in 1584, and could likely have executed this important commission before then. As in all of the large retable projects of the sixteenth century, a variety of craftsmen were concerned—designers, carvers, gilders, painters, *et al.* Pereyns' signature on a predella panel of the lower left implies that he did the large paintings above as well. The carving of the half-columns in the Plateresque manner, the execution of the major bas-relief in the upper center, and the figure sculpture were the product of other, equally skilled hands. It is unfortunate that nineteenth- and twentieth-century modifications of the high altar area have been of an inferior quality to the sixteenth- and eighteenth-century work at Huejotzingo.

LA CATA (Guanajuato)

PILGRIMAGE CHURCH (EL SANTUARIO DEL SEÑOR DE VILLASECA)

The present church dates from about 1725, although the façade and some of the retables were created after 1760. The principal funds for the church fabric came from Don Juan Martínez de Soria and from the owners of the rich Cata mine and that of San Lorenzo. The interior was modified in the nineteenth century.

LA CATA, FAÇADE, EL SANTUARIO (pl. 149)

There is a distinct general relationship of certain major church façades in the Guanajuato area, particularly between those at La Cata and La Valenciana (pl. 153). Both churches were near important mines. The Cata façade is incomplete in its upper sections, and as at La Valenciana there is but one tower. Rather bulky *estípites* dominate both first and second levels of the central portion of the church front; between each pair, however, there is a lush ornamental niche-pilaster, similar to those on the façade at La Valenciana. The dazzling profusion of stepped moldings and foliation over the door derives ultimately from Spanish sources, but neither they nor the *pinjantes* below *estípites* and niche-pilasters were used with such bravura in Spain. Related to the façades of the Sagrario in Mexico City (pl. 95) in its strong horizontal layering and fully developed *estípites*, this façade is probably datable to about 1770—just before the fashion for *rocaille* ornament became dominant in this area (as seen in the façade of the 1780's at La Valenciana).

LAGOS DE MORENO (Jalisco)

PARISH CHURCH (LA PARROQUIA)

This relatively little known and poorly documented church must date from the very end of the eighteenth century. It is, in its main elements, probably not earlier than 1785 and not later than 1795, although the interior was modified in the nineteenth century.

LAGOS DE MORENO, LOWER CENTER OF FAÇADE, LA PARROQUIA (pl. 146)

Among the most graceful creations of the last years of the eighteenth century, the parish church at Lagos de Moreno is undeservedly neglected. In elevation a strikingly tall example of the dramatic twin-towered church of the eighteenth century with high dome and drum over the crossing, it has a most beautifully designed garniture of ornament in the manner of both Guanajuato (side door of San Cayetano de La Valenciana) and San Luis de Potosí (see pls. 154 and 139). The ornamental niche-pilaster is the dominant vertical articulation of the canted wall sections beside the main door, with repeated pilaster echoes behind the ornamented niche. A grand panoply of motifs used in northern Mexico in the decades after 1750 appear here. The down-turned spirals (beneath the figure in the niche and above) as well as the *pinjantes* or lambrequins normally associated with the *estípite;* the plaited capitals of the shallow columns above the niche in the Querétaro style; the scalloped arch above the door related to the side door of the Carmen at San Luis de Potosí; and the flickering appliqué of *rocaille*, seen especially in the empty niches of the second level; all this creates a witchery of Late Baroque and Rococo which rivals the magic combinations of equally complex ornamental sources in such a sixteenth-century façade as San Miguel at Huejotzingo. The towers are more Neo-Classical. On the right side is a fine portal, and a fascinating door farther to the rear which has no other parallel in Mexico.

LA VALENCIANA (Guanajuato)

SAN CAYETANO DE LA VALENCIANA

Begun in 1765, San Cayetano was built with funds from Obregón, owner of La Valenciana mine and later count of that name. It was dedicated on August 6, 1788.

LA VALENCIANA, ENTRANCE STAIRS OF SAN CAYETANO (pl. 152)

These simple, cubist planes of wall have been repeatedly replastered and painted. Today they are a fairly intense rose, which, in the immemorial taste of the folk artists of Mexico, does not clash with the rose-brown stone of the church itself. Situated on a magnificent hillside (actually a level on the side of a mountain), San Cayetano de La Valenciana dominates the once prosperous town—6,000 people in the later eighteenth century—which now has but a few houses, shops, and the residence of the Conde de Rul. Beyond the elaborate wrought iron doorway to the church, one ascends to the small atrium or forecourt which lies before the façade. From here one has views down to Guanajuato, lying in a series of canyons about a mile below, and all of the surrounding mountainous countryside.

LA VALENCIANA, DETAIL, FAÇADE OF SAN CAYETANO
(pl. 153)

This mining magnate's dream church, built to surpass that of Borda in Taxco, was estimated by the *Gaceta de Mexico* of 1788 to have cost 360,000 pesos, an extraordinary sum for the period. Naturally, there had been some inflation throughout the eighteenth century, especially after the silver bonanzas of 1748. Still, the count quite exceeded himself in all details of the edifice. The façade has a date of 1788, ten years after the retables in the apse and transepts inside. Though this inscription refers to the completion of the church—"elaborado, 1788"—it is also roughly a terminal date for façade and tower. The retables, main façade, and side portal are three clear steps in the stylistic developments of the later eighteenth century. The retables with particularly bizarre *estípites* show the gradual overwhelming of structural clarity in the 1770's. By the time the façade was carved, the *estípites* (obviously more tectonic in stone than in the gilded and painted wood inside) were relegated to a wholly subordinate role beside dramatic ornamental niche-pilasters. The whole panoply of the period after 1760 is here—the spirals and *pinjantes*, the stepped moldings and *estípites* of Rodríguez and his circle, the gradual rise to prominence of the ornamental niche-pilaster after its first important use on the Sagrario façades (finished about 1760), and the new fashion of *rocaille* patterns, common after 1775. Even Mudéjar-inspired doors are present in this late, superb pyrotechnical display of craftsmanly elegance and design splendor. Just around the corner to the left, the side door shows the complete triumph of the ornamental niche-pilaster. Only one tower here was completed. Even the color scheme of the church interior (light brown and yellow on white) suggests the very last phase of eighteenth-century design—the Neo-Classical—

which would eventually turn from purely ornamental articulation to the structural formality of columns and pilasters.

LA VALENCIANA, SIDE PORTAL OF SAN CAYETANO
(pl. 154)

If the façade of San Cayetano does for the fashion of the 1780's what Tepotzotlán's façade had done for the fashion of the 1760's, the side portal of San Cayetano represents the exteriorizing of an ornamental sophistication most developed interiorly at Santa Clara and Santa Rosa in Querétaro. There are obvious connections between these brilliant north-central works and those of the capital, Mexico City. Many of the designers must have had training in the metropolis, and then come north to the new-rich communities which provided some of the greatest challenges to their audacity and taste. Yet there is nothing in the capital quite like these interiors and exteriors of the Bajío of north central Mexico and the façades of La Valenciana. For the unprejudiced eye, there is little that surpasses the visual, sensuous vitality of this side portal at San Cayetano. It is not only an incredible piece of design, worthy of Cuvilliés at his best and obviously more than Rococo; it is one of the loveliest pieces of ornamental stone carving of its time. The extreme attenuation of proportions somehow relates to the exhilarating hill setting, as well as reflecting the preference for elongation in the mannered undercurrents of so much mid- and later eighteenth-century Mexican architecture. What often approaches delirium in interior retables (as at Taxco or even here at La Valenciana) is kept miraculously under control in these exterior apotheoses of ornament. The superb doors, with their inevitable geometric paneling, add a piquant contrast to the carved stone around. The portal soars and swoops like an eighteenth-century singer; it breaks into roulades and trills, it throws forth cascades of perfect ornamentation. It is a technical exercise as only that era could do in perfect taste.

LA VALENCIANA, GENERAL VIEW OF REAR OF SAN CAYE-
TANO (pl. 155)

What is most poignantly apparent, after the prodigious technical virtuosity of the church of San Cayetano, is that this is a unique region. With their cacti, barren mountains, and infinite variations of color, the highlands of Mexico have their own geographic and geologic aesthetic, as do all the other distinctive areas of the country. What is seized upon with delight in the remoter areas of Macedonia or Armenia, or in the stark country of central Spain, is rejected in Mexico as "provincial." This curious inability of otherwise deeply sensitive visitors to respond to the special qualities of Mexico make it difficult for the art or the country to be properly understood. It, like the art of Spain or the Byzantine East, is many things at many different times. It can be brilliantly sophisticated, insipidly sophisticated, inspired in its adjustment of sources and interpretations, painfully banal in that same adjustment, folkloristic in a distinguished, creative manner, or cheaply commercial. The viceregal era was almost never the latter; that has been one of the results of nineteenth- and twentieth-century political, social, and economic changes. In the last analysis, however, the modern student or traveler in Mexico is not living in the viceregal age. He or she must bring a complex group of conceptions, attitudes, and prejudices to bear upon what is seen. Certainly the inherent sensibility of builders and decorators to site, to material, and to changes of taste must be apparent; but the end result is a special, involved, and infinitely rewarding process of sympathy for and knowledge of the strengths and weaknesses of Mexican architecture and art. San Cayetano de La Valenciana is an especially compelling example of this.

MARFIL (Guanajuato)

MARFIL, CRUCIFIX (SCULPTURE) (pl. 150)

Among the many figures of the crucified Christ of colonial Mexico, there are a number of particularly important examples, from the *Cristos de caña* of the sixteenth century (made of corn pith paste) to the gruesomely bloodied ones of the eighteenth century. The immediate inspiration for this particular crucifix of *ca.* 1700 is local, but its artistic sources extend far back into the Middle Ages and more directly to the Velásquez painting of Christ based in turn on Montañés' *Christ of Clemency* in Sevilla Cathedral—with the same firm figure and infinitely weary head. It is obvious that a deep spiritual conviction animated the sculptor, for the face is starkly moving.

Among the notable minor arts of the eighteenth and nineteenth century were the tin processional lamps, of which a large number, such as the one here, survive to the present. It is unfortunate that the *pasos* (religious processions) that give Holy Week in Spain its particular quality, especially seen at night with the processional lanterns of silver, have not survived in Mexico; the tin lamps would serve handsomely to illuminate these curious combinations of piety, artistry and drama.

MARFIL, MADONNA (SCULPTURE) (pl. 151)

The dedication or name of the feminine figure here is relatively unimportant; it might be either a Madonna or a saint. (Originally it was a polychromed wooden statue of the eighteenth century with inlaid eyes.) It is rather the configuration of elements which provokes the viewer's aesthetic pleasure—the irregular rubble construction of the wall, the variegated spotting of color in the geraniums around the base of the ruined wooden statue. Certainly these essentially romantic gratifications of a twentieth-century sensibility are far removed from the original intent or appearance of the statue; perhaps, though, they can as effectively suggest the problems of art removed from its original setting to a new aura of associations as they can hint at certain qualities of taste that have consistently controlled Mexican art. These are qualities hard to isolate but relevant to any examination of Mexican art—an indefinable ability to make the casual meaningful and the technically unperfected arresting, as well as a marked feeling for textural relationships and above all for color. These qualities are residual and are usually confined to peripheral areas of a total design, so that the expert craftsmanship and the bravura of organization are more obviously apparent in major works.

MÉXICO (Distrito Federal)

CATHEDRAL OF LA ASUNCIÓN DE MARÍA

The history of the Cathedral of Mexico is complex and still uncertain in some details. Toussaint's monumental *La Catedral de México y el Sagrario Metropolitano* is the most reliable general source. There were two buildings in this area, the *catedral vieja* and the *catedral nueva*. The first was begun about 1524 (dates of 1523, 1524, and 1525 are given by various writers). Work continued into the 1530's, when Fray Juan de Zumárraga finally became bishop (he had arrived in Mexico in 1528) after a period of confusion as to his confirmation, due to difficulties between Spain and the papacy. This "old cathedral" was in the Zócalo, or central space of the old city, just south of the present cathedral's location, and faced west-east. It was a three-aisled church, slightly longer than the present cathedral's width and about 55 feet wide. The nave had octagonal Tuscan pillars, of which a fragment survives as the pedestal for a modern bust of an Indian emperor at the southwest corner of the present atrium. The building, though criticized for its smallness and simplicity, survived until 1624.

The new cathedral was established in 1562 or 1563 (the latter is the more commonly given date). It was *not* on the site of the Aztec pyramids or teocallis, but slightly to the west—within the area of the sacred precinct of pre-Conquest times. It was now oriented south-north (altar at the north). The first campaign of building was directed toward a hall church. The second, under the Spaniard Claudio de Arciniega (in Mexico since 1555 and *maestro mayor* after 1584), was more progressive. This new building began to reflect the centralizing plan tendencies of later sixteenth-century Spanish designs (such as Herrera's plan for Valladolid) as well as the late medieval tendencies of conservative Spanish cathedral design of the earlier sixteenth century. The building eventually became a double clerestoried basilica, with possibly four towers intended, two front and two rear. The elevation was the work of Juan Miguel de Agüero. The names of Alonso Pérez de Castañeda and the Spaniard Juan Gómez de Mora are peripherally associated with the work. Gómez de Mora may have sent a plan, but work had already advanced so far that it was disregarded. The walls and vaults were begun in the sixteenth century and completed by the mid-seventeenth century (1563–1613–1617–1667); dedications were made in 1656 and 1667. After very considerable difficulties with the foundations (because of the water level from the lake of Aztec times), the cathedral was well founded and has experienced less subsidence problems than some

subsequent buildings. The façade was largely completed in the seventeenth century (note a date of 1672 or 1677 on one of the reliefs); it was terminated in the Neo-Classical manner of the later eighteenth and early nineteenth century by the Mexican José Damiáno Ortiz de Castro and the Spaniard Manuel Tolsá—especially the upper parts of the façade and towers and the entire cupola over the crossing (work essentially complete by 1813). The dimensions are about 180 feet wide by about 375 feet long. The towers are just over 200 feet high.

MÉXICO, D. F., VIEW OF CATHEDRAL AND THE SAGRARIO FROM SOUTH SIDE OF ZÓCALO (pl. 94)

Although the great Cathedral of Mexico has a small atrium, the Zócalo is more particularly its forecourt. This has been subjected to many rather accidental or whimsical changes of appearance—at least three since 1900. Currently, the Zócalo is entirely devoid of the fine rows of trees which were planted before the cathedral in the mid-nineteenth century or of the rather sad palms and other vegetation which dated from the 1920's. Attached to the cathedral at the southeast is the Sagrario Metropolitano, a lower structure in the form of a Greek cross with cupola over the intersecting central aisles. This was one of the most influential Mexican buildings of the eighteenth century; designed by Lorenzo Rodríguez, it has the characteristic later colonial Mexico City stone contrast of *tezontle* and *chiluca* (or reddish volcanic pumice and gray-white limestone). The cathedral is almost entirely of limestone. A large-scaled Baroque and Neo-Classical façade for the cathedral is more subtly echoed in the Late Baroque rhythms of the Sagrario. Both emphasize a major central section of their south fronts, with framing elements at the sides —in the case of the cathedral, lofty towers; in the case of the Sagrario, richly decorated side portals. The Sagrario, of course, has two façades—the one to the east can be seen vaguely in this view.

MÉXICO, D. F., INTERIOR OF CATHEDRAL, CROSSING AREA (pl. 96)

The characteristic Spanish cathedral plan of high altar area and *coro* (a major separate area for the choir) in the nave, with a *via de crujía* (processional walk) between, is followed here. The angelic figures supporting candles of the *via de crujía* can be dimly seen in the center of the photograph under the brightest shaft of sunlight; to the right, under the lesser rays of light, is the *coro*, with its magnificent eighteenth-century organ cases. The *coro* was designed by Juan de Rojas, after a competition held in 1696. The *reja* (choir screen) was finished about 1725 and dedicated in 1730. The organs by José Nasarré, finished by Saenz Aragón, were completed *ca.* 1736. The *via de crujía* by José de Lemus dates from 1743–1745. The metal used in the *via de crujía* balustrades and *reja* is an unusual semiprecious alloy (*tumbaga*) and is documented as having been made in Macao. Above all of this eighteenth-century work rise the arcades of nave and aisle chapels, with clerestories and vaults over them; the nave vaults are more medievalizing; the aisle domical vaults more Renaissance. There are sixteen important chapels in the cathedral, with one of the most complete surveys of retable design, painting, and sculpture possible in colonial Mexico.

MÉXICO, D. F., NORTH END OF CATHEDRAL, WITH ALTAR (*Retablo*) DE LOS REYES (pl. 97)

Among the grand and important retable commissions of the eighteenth century, the Altar (Retablo) de los Reyes must take first place. It set the stage for the virtuoso size and complexity of the retable ensembles at Tepotzotlán, Taxco, and Valenciana, among others. Designed by the Spaniard, Gerónimo Balbás, it was executed between 1718 and 1737 at a cost of 18,000 pesos. The gilding was by the painter, Francisco Martínez (1743) and the paintings included in the retable were by Juan Rodríguez Juárez. Justino Fernández has given a full account of its history, iconography, and critical reception in his *El Retablo de los Reyes*. It was a crucial work in the creation of enthusiasm for the *estípite* and the ornamental language of the mid-eighteenth century. Balbás had designed an almost exactly similar work (now destroyed) for the Sagrario of the Cathedral of Sevilla. His demonstration of the deep, cavelike space of Late Baroque retables (also used by José de Churriguera)—with the *estípite* in place of the *salomónica* —undoubtedly helped influence a number of the hollow-curve façades of the eighteenth century. However, Mexico was essentially unresponsive to this kind of deep, curved space, and the younger Spaniard, Lorenzo Rodríguez, took many of the ornamental ideas of Balbás, as well as those of Francisco Hurtado and his circle in Granada, for his more immediately influential planar Sagrario façades. The ornamental vocabulary of Balbás and of the Hurtado circle was given a special new statement by Rodríguez which was to echo through Mexico for forty years. Only one section of this great retable can be seen in the photograph, to the right. In the center of the photograph—to the left side of the apse space—is one of a pair of quasi-retables (actually paintings framed in elaborate carved wood panels) which conclusively date the popularity of the Rococo in Mexico. Their execution in 1774–1775, using glittering, irregular shell fragments of *rocaille*, marked a new era in fashion. Gerónimo Balbás also designed the *ciprés* (canopy) of the high altar of the Cathedral of Mexico, which was repaired by Isidoro Vicente de Balbás and later disappeared.

SAGRARIO METROPOLITANO

The parish of the area near the Cathedral of Mexico was administered up to the eighteenth century in a large room of the cathedral. Plans for a Sagrario were discussed in 1693 and again in 1701; they were more formally stated in 1728. The first stone of the new building seems to have been laid in February, 1749, although construction did not effectively begin until 1750. Lorenzo Rodríguez was the architect, and the Cofradía del Santísimo Sacramento was the sponsoring agency. The façades (*portadas*) were largely finished by 1759, and Rodríguez left the project for other, new commissions in 1760. The dedication date was February 6, 1768. Before the end of the eighteenth century there were two fires—a slight one in 1776 and a serious one in 1796, although not everything was destroyed in the latter. More deleterious to the interior were the fashion-motivated changes of the nineteenth century in many of the retables. (The *retablo mayor* is by Pedro Patiño Ixtolinque, a pupil of Tolsá.) Earthquake damage occurred in 1858 and 1895. The Sagrario, long closed for repairs, has once again been opened provisionally, although the interior has temporary walls which obstruct old perspectives. The building is about 145 feet by 156 feet and 132 feet high at the cupola.

MÉXICO, D. F., SOUTH FAÇADE, EL SAGRARIO (pl. 95)
Although there is a slight difference between the south and the east façades of the Sagrario (the east façade is probably later, is a little more damaged, and has generally finer figure sculpture), they are essentially the same. In them is the most important statement of two new aspects of mid- and later eighteenth-century façade and retable design: the *estípite* and the ornamental niche-pilaster. The *estípites* in the first level are rather bulky; those in the second level are more elongated. Below, between the massive, salient *estípites* is a distinctive ornamental niche-pilaster. (Kubler has mistakenly called them intercolumnar *estípites*; there is no aspect of an *estípite* pilaster to these completely unarchitectural but articulating massings of ornament around a niche.) In the second level, there are broad and narrow niche-pilasters. Lorenzo Rodríguez continued to confine his decorative and articulative elements to two strong horizontal layers (albeit providing Late Baroque interpenetration in the stepped molding, like an eighteenth century *alfiz*, and broken pediment, which rise over the door). Furthermore, the entire central section of the façade is clamped rigidly into an area bounded by simple, projecting buttress-pilasters at the sides of the carved *estípites* and the complex yet masterfully controlled richness of ornamental parts. Linking the delimited central section of the façade to ornamented doors at either side are wall sections in *tezontle* with a delicate upper molding—curved and stepped from high to low, and echoed in the wave-like rhythm of the curved moldings over the upper center of the façade. In his return to a more traditional regularity of basic façade design (that is, in the central sections), Rodríguez asserted once again the conservative character of much eighteenth-century work, which often followed the regular horizontal layers of retables and façades of the "academic" type. Master of accent and color that he was, the end result is a superb adjustment of progressive and conservative trends—profoundly Mexican in color and organization rather than Spanish. It would be impossible to evaluate fully the influence of these façades. Indeed scholars are still debating the attribution of works in the city and province to both Lorenzo and his circle. It would probably be no exaggeration, however, to call

Rodríguez the most powerful force of the eighteenth century. The extraordinary fact appears to be that he arrived in Mexico with less experience than has commonly been assumed, worked at the Mint, and through marriage to the daughter of a powerful architect gradually ingratiated himself with major patrons. He was certainly a genius of design, and, though he borrowed in whole or part from others, his final synthesis was unique.

SAN FERNANDO

This fine church, facing Avenida Hidalgo on the Plaza de Guerrero in Mexico City, was built by the friars of San Fernando, an order founded in Mexico City in 1693. The first stone was laid on October 11, 1735, and the building was opened on April 19th or 20th, 1755. Badly shaken by the earthquake of 1858, it was repaired in 1859–1861. The church adjoins an historic cemetery, the Panteón de San Fernando, where Benito Juárez is buried.

MÉXICO, D. F., FAÇADE OF SAN FERNANDO (pl. 93)

A carved stone façade is flanked by tower bases in *tezontle*. In design it is a perfect example of a basic façade type of the later seventeenth and eighteenth century—an arched door flanked by columns or half-columns, a second level with didactic or tutelary relief flanked by four more vertical members, and a third-story window with lesser ornamental repeats of the vertical members below. Hovering between the fashion for *salomónicas* and *estípites*, this façade has the curious wavy, fluted Tuscan half-columns in the first story which are associated with other early eighteenth-century Mexico City façades. A minor concession to Baroque receding and projecting movement occurs in the canted niches of the first level which lead the eye out and forward from the sides. The ornament, aside from the decoration of the *estípites*, is rather simple, and still Renaissance-Baroque in vocabulary.

FORMER BALVANERA CHAPEL OF MONASTIC CHURCH OF SAN FRANCISCO (NOW CAPILLA DE LA SANTA ESCALA)

The great Franciscan monastery in Mexico City, founded soon after the Conquest, gradually increased in size until it occupied many city blocks in the eighteenth century (including a church, eleven chapels, and nine monastic dormitories). Although the church of San Francisco was finished by 1716, the Balvanera chapel (dedicated to the Virgin of Balvanera) received a new façade about 1770 or 1775. Following the Reform laws of 1860, the monastic group was gradually destroyed. In 1868, some of the remaining structures were sold to the American Bishop Riley, for his revival of the Mozarabic liturgy (the Christian rite used in Spain until the twelfth century) in that variant of the Episcopal or Anglican church called the "Catholic Church of America." At that time, statues of the Virgin, Santo Domingo, and San Antonio were taken down and some reliefs (including one of the stigmatization of St. Francis in the upper center) were destroyed on the façade of the Balvanera chapel. The property was later reacquired by the Roman Catholic church; in 1952, the Friars Minor were considering restoring the façade, but to date no action has been taken.

MÉXICO, D. F., LOWER CENTRAL SECTION OF FAÇADE, FORMER BALVANERA CHAPEL OF SAN FRANCISCO (pl. 98)

The attribution and dating of this façade are still uncertain. Some authorities date it to 1790. It would appear more reasonably to have been designed about ten years after the Sagrario façades, and might be a later work of Lorenzo Rodríguez himself. Typical stylistic mark of his work is the combination of ornamental vocabulary and design; rustication (in niches here), *estípites*, ornamental niche-pilasters, spirals, and a lush foliation—now pushing beyond the tectonic character of the Sagrario façades into the articulated non-architecture of the period between 1770 and 1790. The relationship of levels is more complex, but the area over the mixtilinear arched door with its stepped moldings, niche, and semicircular broken pediment is close to the Sagrario façades. Whoever the master was, this is one of the best façades of the later eighteenth century in Mexico City. Behind that façade today are other chapels and the renovated church of San Francisco.

SAN JUAN DE DÍOS

The present eighteenth-century church occupies the general area where Doctor Pedro López erected the early hospital of Nuestra Señora de los Desampara-

dos; it would seem likely that the hospital chapel was on the site of the more recent church. In 1604, five Franciscan friars arrived in Mexico City to found a monastery, and were given charge of the hospital on February 25, 1604. A new church was dedicated on May 16, 1729. On March 10, 1776 (1766?), a serious fire caused extensive damage which was later repaired.

MÉXICO, D. F., FAÇADE OF SAN JUAN DE DÍOS (pl. 92)

The concave façade of San Juan de Díos by Miguel Custodio Durán is one of a number of such fronts in eighteenth-century Mexico. Their cavelike space is a fairly timid parallel of the deep curved space of Balbás' Altar (Retablo) de los Reyes (pl. 97); it is significant that no major façade was designed this way. The immutable rectilinearism of Mexican façades, modified with canted sides or center section, with Baroque projections and recessions, and so on, was rarely changed for this curved façade type. Angulo cites Spanish precedents for Durán's design; it was partly influenced by them to be sure, but one also feels (aside from the retable source suggested earlier) that it represented an eighteenth-century equivalent of the open chapel, particularly the curved side façade of the Third Order at Cuernavaca's Franciscan ensemble. The undulant pilasters of the first level here are extended in a series of flame-like undulant obelisks in the second. Absence of a firm entablature above the second level aids in expanding this wavy movement into the rayed canopy which crowns the façade; undulant pilasters in the tower augment the change from vertical to pseudo-spiral. The whole design, however, is cautious and tentative rather than assertive. Handsome Mudéjar-inspired plaster ornament on the tower base and right side of the façade, as well as on the wall of the neighboring hospital portal, continue the infinitely varied geometry of Islam into the Late Baroque. The little plaza in the foreground once was the center of a flourishing funeral flower market; its morbid fantasy has been banished to make way for a more healthful, if less vivid, planting.

SANTO DOMINGO

On the Plaza Santo Domingo (or Plaza 23 de Mayo), the present church was dedicated on August 3, 1736, replacing a structure of the sixteenth century which was ruined by a flood in 1716. (Some writers give a consecration date of 1754 for the church; this may refer to a single chapel.) The tower is *ca.* 1732. The Dominicans were in Mexico by 1526, and their early church here was on the site of the later colonial University School of Medicine (now moved to the new University campus in the Pedregal); the site of the present church is to the west, on part of the older monastic property.

MÉXICO, D. F., RELIEF FROM CENTER OF SECOND LEVEL, FAÇADE OF SANTO DOMINGO (pl. 90)

The church of Santo Domingo was in Pedro de Arrieta's hands just before 1720. The façade, though closely related to certain of his works (La Profesa in Mexico City and the Basilica of Guadalupe), has a few more progressive tendencies than he revealed in his early work—such as *estípite* pilasters in the top level and the *pinjante* or lambrequin. (De Arrieta died in great poverty in 1738, two years after the dedication of Santo Domingo.) The large relief of the Descent of the Holy Spirit on Santo Domingo de Guzmán, while Peter and Paul look on, is not one of the sculptural masterpieces of the eighteenth century; the transfer of a print or painting source to a relief has none of the verve of the sixteenth-century works of this type. The eared frame around the relief was a form common to the seventeenth century. The dry execution of this molding as well as the foliation on the surrounding surfaces reveals the rather dull character of much earlier eighteenth-century work in Mexico City—entirely lacking the imaginative, if less "correct," carving of such eared frames and foliation in Oaxaca. It is partly the crisp potential of the stone; later it will admirably suit the prismatic hardness of the *estípite* era. At this time, it serves to only accentuate the Baroque academism of these façades.

MÉXICO, D. F., SAN AGUSTÍN (SCULPTURE), LOWER LEFT SIDE OF FAÇADE OF SANTO DOMINGO (pl. 91)

The first level of Santo Domingo's façade is distinctly more interesting than the second. Undulant fluting, in the manner of Miguel Custodio Durán, animates the Corinthian three-quarter columns; their lower sections are covered with a beautifully executed pattern of foliation and fruit. A rather naïve accent of

color is achieved with the tiled cross of Alcántara (one of the Dominican insignia) above the niche in which San Agustín is holding a church. Altogether, the adjustment of discreet rustication and foliation here, with the *movementé* animation of the undulating fluting, gives the lower level of Santo Domingo's façade a very different total effect from the second, suggesting that Arrieta may have planned the drier second level, and Custodio Durán, the first, with over-all supervision of the work by Custodio Durán. Of course, it may well be attributable to the difference in craftsmen.

MORELIA (Michoacán)

CATHEDRAL OF LA TRANSFIGURACIÓN DE CRISTO

The first cathedral of Michoacán (for the famous Bishop Don Vasco de Quiroga) was at Tzintzuntzán (in use after 1537). Don Vasco later transferred his building enthusiasms to Pátzcuaro, projecting the construction of an extraordinary cathedral with five converging naves. In 1579, the episcopal seat was transferred to Morelia, then called Valladolid. Situated between the present Plazas de la Paz and de los Mártires, the great seventeenth- and eighteenth-century trachyte Cathedral of Morelia replaced an earlier structure of wood and adobe. This first cathedral was in a ruinous condition by 1654, and was repaired but again fell into ruin by 1671. A plan for the new cathedral was approved in 1660. The principal architect of this early period was Vicente Barroso de la Escayola (died 1694), assisted by Pedro de Guedea. There was an important campaign of building in 1672–1674, and again after 1683. Various architects became *maestro mayor* later: Juan de Silva, Juan de Cepeda, and Lucas Durán. The cathedral was dedicated on May 10, 1705. The façade continued later; it was in progress by 1717, and the towers were finished in 1744 under Bishops Calatayud and Matos Coronado. Annexes (1765) were executed during the bishopric of Sánchez de Tagle. The interior was modified in 1844 with a new color scheme, and many of the interior fittings and silver were despoiled about 1858.

MORELIA, GENERAL VIEW OF CATHEDRAL (pl. 122)

Seen from a rooftop to the northwest of the cathedral (which faces north), the lofty towers (about 200 feet high) of slightly lighter pink stone than the main fabric rise over the twin plazas of Morelia. These plazas are creations of the mid-nineteenth century, and the regularity of the spaces now flanking the cathedral, as well as the fine cast metal fence (1854), give the whole area an order that was not present in the seventeenth and eighteenth century. The tiled dome of the Cathedral of Morelia is a striking contrast to the uniform color of this immense and majestic building, which is probably the most stylistically consistent cathedral of its size in Mexico. The arcaded *portales* of the surrounding buildings, the presence of a university, as well as the essentially dignified character of the town's architecture gives Morelia a suggestion of old Salamanca in Spain. It is one of the few Mexican towns which forcibly evoke Hispanic comparisons, but the details are entirely Mexican.

MORELIA, FAÇADE OF CATHEDRAL (pl. 123)

In its massing, with a pair of very high towers flanking a façade in three sections—rising from lower side sections to a higher central section—the Cathedral of Morelia is generically related to the Cathedral of Puebla. Both have a colored fabric. Morelia is pink or rose; Puebla is gray, which is used to advantage to set off façade reliefs of white. Both are essentially sober in their ornamental details, and reflect an underlying classicism which rests firmly beneath a Mannerist or Baroque surface. Since Morelia's façade was executed in the eighteenth century, it began to manifest not only the continuing classicism of that era (especially seen in Mexico City, in de Arrieta's work) but the advent of the *estípite* and its related ornament. There are *pinjantes* or lambrequins hanging just under the Ionic capitals of the pilasters which frame the central door. They are multiplied under the figure niches and occur under pilaster capitals on the sides of the main façade and towers. *Estípite* pilasters are present in the top level center and side. The principal bas-relief above the main door has a mixtilinear arch above it, and the upper part of the entire façade writhes in a curvetting of broken cornices and stepped moldings which mirror the growth of this animating principle in Mexico City. However, like the somewhat later Sagrario, the façade here respects the firm compartmentalization of the seven-

teenth century; center and sides are divided by pier buttresses. The whole is elegant, sober, and yet of its time.

MORELIA, TOWER OF CATHEDRAL (pl. 124)

The towers were the last completed part of the main fabric of the cathedral. Curiously, they are not so much of their time as the façade. Were it not for the polygonal arches in the first level (with a "pushed-up" cornice over a blank stone area above these arches) and the *pinjantes* or lambrequins under the Tuscan capitals of the paneled pilasters and over the triglyphs of the frieze, one could almost call this design Neo-Classical, and date these towers to 1810 —especially with their massive urns on squared pedestals.

LA MERCED

In 1604, Pedro de Burgos and Alonso García bought the house of Melchor Pardo and María de Ortega to found a Mercedarian monastery. The building advanced slowly during the seventeenth century, and the church was not completed until 1736. In 1908, the interior was redecorated by Teofano López.

MORELIA, SIDE PORTAL OF LA MERCED (pl. 125)

The relatively pure use of classical detail on this portal—the fine Tuscan pilasters, the simple entablature above, the pediment broken only by a Mercedarian escutcheon—might place this within the Italian sixteenth century. However, the magnificent carved wooden doors, with their geometric paneling of the Mudéjar persuasion, filled with foliation that might be Renaissance or Baroque, immediately place this ensemble in the Hispanic world, and more specifically in Mexico of the earlier eighteenth century. The principal façade of La Merced has a group of clumsy, bulky *estípites* and is altogether removed in spirit from this tranquil, carefully balanced portal on the present Calle Nacional or Real.

LAS ROSAS (SANTA ROSA DE LIMA)

On the site of an old Catherinist convent, founded in 1590, Las Rosas lies on land bought in 1738 by Bishop Matos Coronado. It was begun in 1746 while

Martín Elizacoechea was bishop, and dedicated in 1757, following its completion in the preceding year. Attached to the conventual church is the Colegio de Santa Rosa.

MORELIA, GENERAL VIEW OF LAS ROSAS FROM PLAZA DE LAS ROSAS (pl. 126)

Typical of the eighteenth-century nuns' churches, Las Rosas has twin portals on the flank of the building. A street façade is animated with pier buttresses, echoing in part the interior divisions of the church. The dome is relatively simple, and continues the sobriety of ornamental detail forcibly enunciated for Morelia in the cathedral.

MORELIA, UPPER LEVELS OF THE PAIRED FAÇADES OF LAS ROSAS (pl. 127)

The carving of architectural and sculptural adornment of these twin façades is slightly less sophisticated than that of the cathedral façades, but it has a clarity and piquant combination of the serious and light-hearted which is ingratiating. The Ionic pilasters are correct, but a little stubby in proportion. The frieze above is lightly touched with cross-hatching—delicately animating this section. Beside the windows are caryatids which turn into cascades of foliation and prepare one for the dramatically enlarged caryatid-cornucopias of the later eighteenth-century Mexican retables (such as the transept retables at San Agustín, Salamanca, Mexico). Below the window on the left is the Madonna and Child, flanked by a saint and angel; on the right is a rather different interpretation of the Annunciation with the Child already present in the center. Under the stepped gables in the manner of Alonso Cano are medallions with (left, San Fermín and San Francisco Xavier; right, San Martín and Santa Teresa of Ávila), and various saints beneath a God the Father and a Holy Dove. There is something a little childlike in these compositions, or perhaps reflective of the fancywork which the sisters might have made the convent. The general spirit here is early eighteenth century, with the *pinjantes* or lambrequins beneath the Ionic pilasters to suggest the mid-century, when the façades were actually carved. There are a few eighteenth-century retables inside the church, although most of the décor is in a wan nineteenth-century taste.

MUSEUM

The museum of Morelia—one of the most tastefully planned provincial galleries in the country—is housed in the Casa de Don Isidoro Huarte, father-in-law of Emperor Iturbide. It was built *ca.* 1755, with an upper story added in 1775. The materials for the structure are said to have come from the stone left over from the fine aqueduct of Morelia. The house later passed to other private owners, and then to a girls' school; it has been reworked interiorly to fit it for a museum.

MORELIA, HEAD OF CHRIST (SCULPTURE) IN MUSEUM (pl. 128)

With much of the same compulsive realism as the famous seventeenth-century head of San Juan de Díos in the Religious Museum of Mexico City, this head of Christ (or Man of Sorrows) with the crown of thorns is probably a little later in date. The half-opened mouth (occasionally in the seventeenth century with human teeth) and the vitreous eyes give the head a vacuous terror, which perfectly embodies physical pain bordering on the semiconscious. The facial type is more Mexican than that of the Dolorosa in this same museum.

MORELIA, SORROWING MADONNA (SCULPTURE) IN MUSEUM (pl. 129)

This sorrowing Madonna of carved and gilded wood (in the *estofado* technique) shows the skill of Mexican sculptors of the period just before 1700, when the deeply felt pathos of the Late Baroque was moving into the suavity of the eighteenth century. Inspired by the work of Gregorio Fernández, Montañés, and Cano in Spain, the figure is very fine. Over a carved wooden figure, plaster of Paris (gesso) and linen were molded to form the undercoating for gilding and polychromy. Gold was applied to the garment areas, covered with color for the pattern, and picked or engraved to give greater variety to the surface. Hands and face were given a special, fine coating of polychromy called *encarnación*. Eyes were often of semiprecious stones to heighten the vitality or expressiveness of the figure.

OAXACA (Oaxaca)

CATHEDRAL OF LA ASUNCIÓN DE LA VIRGEN

The Cathedral of Oaxaca was founded in 1535 (built to 1544 and later) and rebuilt between 1702–1730 under Bishop Maldonado and Señor Francisco Santiago Calderón after a disastrous series of earthquakes ending in 1674. The *Gaceta de México* (1728) refers to the impending completion of the cathedral. The towers were added by 1733, and the cathedral was reconsecrated on July 12. It has been shaken by earthquakes since, and repaired. The interior with its three aisles and fine *coro* has suffered despoliation and revision. Fortunately, the unpleasant twentieth-century clock tower on the façade has recently been partly removed.

OAXACA, LOWER CENTER OF FAÇADE OF CATHEDRAL (pl. 86)

Although it is not evident in this detail, the design of the façade of the Cathedral of Oaxaca, facing the Alameda or Plaza Principal, represents a gradual amalgamation of the once rigidly separated triple sections of the great Mexican cathedral façades (like Mexico and Puebla). The entire central section is advanced forward beyond the recessive sections over the lesser doors of the main façade. Of the designer, it is known only that Pedro de Arrieta gave suggestions for the church's completion, which the viceroy ordered to be followed. Vaguely related in the projecting central section, with its canted edges, to de Arrieta's façade for the Basilica at Guadalupe (1709), the façade of the Cathedral of Oaxaca is nevertheless a more attractive whole than Guadalupe. Much of the beauty of this Oaxacan façade lies in the soft green-brown stone used in the area, sometimes almost pistachio in color and at other times more beige. The incredible proliferation of ornament in this material gives the eighteenth-century Oaxacan façades their special flavor—but it is a proliferation restrained by the severe classicism of the columnar forms and the marked horizontality of organization. Notable is the filigree of carving which ornaments the bases of columns, the pedestals of figures in niches, the arches, frames, and base supports. The sculpture is not dazzling, but it has a quiet ease and

gravity that makes it a worthy adjunct to the balance between architecture and decoration here.

OAXACA, ASSUMPTION OF VIRGIN (RELIEF), FAÇADE OF CATHEDRAL (pl. 87)

Most of these reliefs were inspired by prints, translated into stone carving. They have, thus, a didactic quality which relieves them from the critical standards of great original and symbolic Baroque sculpture in the round, conceived as such from the beginning. In the present work, aside from the reserved expressiveness of the disciples, the Christ, God the Father, and Mary with attendant cherubs, the most technically interesting feature of the carving is the chevron-sharp patterning of drapery folds behind Mary, and the wavelike cloudlets which remind us of those used later on wooden retables. Almost overpowering the relief proper is a superb "eared" frame, with moldings covered in a surprisingly thoughtful variety of ornamental enrichment—from Classically inspired egg-and-dart and dentil to freer foliate patterns. Purists may find this inventive combination of old and new excessive; but for the devotee of the Oaxacan style, this is a miraculously exciting adjustment of plain and complex.

OAXACA, DETAIL OF A PANEL BENEATH A FIGURE NICHE, FIRST LEVEL, FAÇADE OF CATHEDRAL (pl. 88)

In some instances the foliation twines about a grotesque face, which the indigenists might wish to assume had "Indian" characteristics. Rather, like the foliate ornament itself, the source must have been some engravings of the sixteenth or early seventeenth century, particularly the fantasy prints of the Northern Mannerists of Germany and Flanders.

OAXACA, DETAIL OF PEDESTAL, FAÇADE OF CATHEDRAL (pl. 89)

The pedestals of the Corinthian half-columns in the first level of the façade at the Cathedral of Oaxaca (that is, the blocks beneath the column bases) are ornamented with involved foliate patterns. This detail allows one to see how the weathering of the relatively soft stone has given the work a certain rough granulation which enhances its quality—reminding the traveler of the worn and richly carved façades of

Lecce, Italy, in an equally soft material, or of carvings in the late Roman world of the Near East.

PILGRIMAGE CHURCH (EL SANTUARIO DE LA SOLEDAD)

The Santuario de la Soledad was originally dedicated to San Sebastián, but due to a miracle it was transferred to the Virgen de la Soledad. The miracle is said to have taken place during the time of Bishop Bohorques (1617–1673), and the pilgrimage church was consecrated by Bishop Sariñana on September 6, 1690. Wilder Weismann dates the façade to 1682–1690, and considers it later than the church itself. The *Gaceta de México* (May, 1732) refers to the departure of a religious group from Mexico City in 1697 to establish the *convento* of Nuestra Senora de la Soledad, erected at the expense of Don Pedro de Otarola.

OAXACA, FAÇADE OF SANTUARIO DE LA SOLEDAD (pl. 83)

Various sources are suggested for this unusual, angled façade design on Avenida Independencia facing the Jardín Socrates. Obviously it is related to a retable of the type seen at Santo Domingo in Puebla (1688). Toussaint compares it to the façade of the University of Oñate in Spain. It is also related to the abbey church of Sainte Amande in France (1624–1633), although the French work has more stories. A retable precedent is the most likely immediate source. Classicizing three-quarter columns in the first two levels (Tuscan and Ionic) are followed with helicoid columns in the third level and classicist pilasters in the fourth, top level, framing a Virgin of the Immaculate Conception at the apex of the design. The Virgen de la Soledad is represented in the second level relief, center, while other saints fill the niches. The carving would seem to be by the workshop whose later members did San Agustín's façade (Oaxaca). Towers, though fairly high and covered with tile domes, are pushed back into lesser importance behind this bold, screenlike façade. The church interior has some large paintings and a fine stucco vault over the presbytery.

SAN AGUSTÍN

This church on Calles Guerrero and Armenta y López was finished in 1722.

OAXACA, SAN AGUSTÍN (RELIEF), FAÇADE OF SAN AGUSTÍN (pl. 84)

The beautifully carved high relief panel is closely related to a similar one on the façade of the former church of San Agustín in Mexico City—now the National Library. Both are based on a common graphic art source in the sixteenth century, representing Augustine (standing on three heads), holding a church and protecting monks of his order under his cloak, which is held up by young angels. As Wilder Weismann has so well demonstrated, the Oaxacan relief is more naturalistic and less correctly hieratic than that of Mexico City; and yet, as she notes (*Mexico in Sculpture*, p. 99): "one finds oneself constantly siding with the less correct in favor of vitality and even ingenuousness of statement, more interested in the provincial artist who is screwed up to the highest pitch of his capacities than in the metropolitan sculptor who has competently learned his lesson." In this particular instance the "provincial" artist has handled the technical details of carving as well as the "metropolitan," and has gone far beyond the metropolitan in the grace of framing the relief proper and the ornamental character of the carving on frieze above and columns to the side. It is but one more warning to avoid the categorical distinction of "provincial" and "metropolitan" in Mexico, where within a local style there are masters of varying degrees of conception and accomplishment.

OAXACA, SAN JUAN EVANGELISTA (SCULPTURE), FAÇADE OF SAN AGUSTÍN (pl. 85)

The powerfully conceived figure of St. John the Evangelist carrying the chalice is almost Flemish or Germanic in physical type, and bears very little relation to the people who must have carved the figure. The inscription in the cartouche below is dated August, 1699, suggesting that the façade sculpture here probably was executed about ten or, by extension, twenty years after the work at La Soledad—spanning the time between La Soledad and the cathedral façades. There is still the restraint of seventeenth-century work in Oaxaca about this façade—with its clear-cut levels and quadripartite composition. The combination of strapwork and foliate patterns on the lower parts of the columns shows the strong persistence of Mannerist strap interlaces exteriorly, as they could be seen interiorly (especially at Santo Domingo) in Oaxaca towards the end of the seventeenth century. There is an interesting *retablo mayor* inside San Agustín which may have been pieced together from smaller parts.

Santo Domingo

Santo Domingo in Oaxaca was begun in 1575 by Fray Hernando Cavarcos and completed close to 1675 (the exact terminal date is not known). It is one of the very few true cryptocollateral churches in Mexico (that is one, which from the exterior seems to be a basilica, is actually a single nave church with deep chapels). The extraordinarily massive walls and generally heavy construction of this building, as well as the adjacent Dominican monastery with its fine cloister, reveals its earthquake country setting. On the Plaza del Rosario near Calle Juárez, Santo Domingo is surrounded with an iron fence surmounted with the same iron angels which appear around the Cathedral of Puebla's atrium. The interior stucco work of both church and Capilla del Rosario is important; that of the nave dates from 1657, while that of the chapel was finished in 1729. The enormous cost of Santo Domingo, mentioned by writers since Baxter (his estimate was 13,000,000 pesos), seems to be based on hearsay evidence. Some of the seventeenth and eighteenth century retables were destroyed— notably the *retablo mayor,* originally of 1612, replaced in 1681 and again in the nineteenth century.

OAXACA, FAÇADE OF SANTO DOMINGO (pl. 59)

This façade may date later than the church fabric's completion, although sometime about 1675 seems a reasonable date for it. The organization of levels, with paired columns framing niches, with a relief above the arched door, and above that a window in the third level, is typical of Mexico City in the later seventeenth and early eighteenth century, with certain variations. Here everything is squeezed into a tall, narrow space between forbiddingly heavy tower bases. The poor integration of the relief with its background, the essentially "extra" character of the fourth level of the façade with its figures against empty walls, and the heavy and rather crude character of the sculpture inevitably suggest an intermediate

stage leading toward the finesse of San Agustín and the more elaborate cathedral façades in Oaxaca. Still, there is a kind of sturdy concision and forthrightness about Santo Domingo which is happily reinforced in the classicist towers with their tile domes and cupolas.

OAXACA, STUCCOED VAULT UNDER CHOIR OF SANTO DOMINGO (pl. 60)

This delightful Tree of Jesse (it was erroneously identified as the lineage of Santo Domingo by an early writer) represents the continuity of the Pueblan interior stucco tradition farther south into Oaxaca. Wilder Weismann suggests that this may be the earliest work of the master stuccoists in this church (1625?). It is a unique recreation in Mexico of a Biblical family history common in the medieval era in Europe; there is nothing here of the mannered strapwork patterns common in the nave. The whole ensemble breathes an air of naïve naturalism; the grapes look as if they came from modern California, and the graceful half-figures, on flower pedestals, out of some Renaissance game of chess.

OAXACA, VAULT SECTION ADJACENT TO TREE OF JESSE UNDER CHOIR OF SANTO DOMINGO (pl. 61)

The strapwork patterns, the spirals, the crimped edge cut-out plate forms—obviously inspired by metal prototypes—represent another phase of stucco decoration, more closely related to the nave vaults of Santo Domingo, Puebla. Most of these vault surfaces have been restored and repainted; particularly, here, the gilding, white plaster surfaces, and polychromy, with the names of Dominican missionaries over the figures on the piers, have been freshened in the eighteenth and nineteenth centuries. Fortunately, the restorers did not use the tinselly tones which pass for colonial taste in some parts of the interior of Santa Maria Tonantzintla (pl. 109).

OAXACA, DOME OF CAPILLA DEL ROSARIO, SANTO DOMINGO (pl. 62)

The Capilla del Rosario, finished in 1729, was dedicated in 1731; its construction took seven years. It was richly decorated with gilded and polychromed stucco, somewhat less perfect in craftsmanship than that of the nave of the church. The slight irregularities are still attractive, despite the undoubted restoration which has been effected here. However, the spiritual content of the protective Virgin and of the saints is diluted compared to the seventeenth-century figures in the church; they are agreeable but insipid. The whole work suggests adequate provincialism, which was certainly not true of the nave and vault under the *coro*—sometimes naïve, but never merely adequate. The glitter of gold, the swirled marshmallow cloudlets, and an array of ornament forms (including some classical paterae that look like sunflowers) make the Capilla del Rosario's dome bright and festive; it is also a little hectic and more than a little superficial.

OAXACA, EVANGELIST MATTHEW FROM A PENDENTIVE OF THE DOME, CAPILLA DEL ROSARIO, SANTO DOMINGO (pl. 63)

On each pendentive of the dome of the Capilla del Rosario at Oaxaca is an evangelist. Like the Triumph of Mary in the dome itself, they are suggestive of a more mundane character in the religion of the eighteenth century. The four evangelists are functionaries rather than inspired scribes; weighed down by their lavish robes they seem more worried than ecstatic, especially since they are rather precariously balanced on the wings of small cherubs! The Capilla del Rosario is close to folk art, but it lacks the spark of great folk art. It is charming, local work, using past precedent and techniques for a very passable execution and very lively feast of color. It points up the importance of more carefully weighing the difference between routine works in a distinguished tradition, inspired provincialism, and folk art. The difference is important for colonial Mexico.

OCOTLÁN (Tlaxcala): see Taxco, Santa Prisca (notes for pl. 117)

OZUMBA (Mexico)

PARISH CHURCH (LA PARROQUIA)

Formerly a Franciscan monastic foundation (after 1585), Ozumba's parish church has a façade and tower of the late seventeenth century (1697), with other work of the eighteenth century.

OZUMBA, DOOR, LA PARROQUIA (pl. 113)

There are dozens of these fine Mudéjar-inspired wooden doors in eighteenth-century Mexico. It would be difficult to date them exactly, but these appear to be about 1740 or 1750, just before the vogue for *rocaille* motifs became apparent. The weathered foliation of the recessed panels, the massive iron nailheads (more bosses than nails) could be paralleled in almost any part of the viceroyalty. These doors provide an unfailing order and at the same time an exotic undertone of an Islamic past, in the rich adventures among more elaborate European ornamental sources of the mid- and later eighteenth-century church façades.

PÁTZCUARO (Michoacán)

Pátzcuaro is one of the most venerable colonial towns in Mexico. Founded early in the sixteenth century, and the particular pride of its beloved Don Vasco de Quiroga—the influential first bishop of Michoacán—Pátzcuaro has a number of important buildings of the viceregal era. Its churches are generally devoid of any interior features of great importance, and most are of the greatest simplicity exteriorly, with the notable exception of the Basilica.

PÁTZCUARO, VIEW TO SAN AGUSTÍN (pl. 121)

San Agustín was a sixteenth-century foundation, but the present building was revised into the seventeenth century, and the unfinished tower dates from the eighteenth. (Sr. González Galván of the Instituto de Investigaciones Estéticas at the National University has prepared plans which will permit its completion as originally intended.) Entirely reworked interiorly, the structure has become a library in the twentieth century—like San Agustín in Mexico City—a not unfitting though unanticipated use of structures which belonged to the most studious of the sixteenth-century monastic orders. In the distance, Lake Pátzcuaro can be seen over the roofs of the town, which contribute much to the special effect of this still unspoiled colonial "museum." (The suggestion of asphalting the cobbled streets of Pátzcuaro in 1960 brought protests from all enthusiasts of the viceregal era.)

PUEBLA (Puebla)

Cathedral of La Immaculada Concepción de María Santísima

The earliest cathedral in Puebla was begun in 1536 and finished in 1539; it had three aisles and a roof of straw. This provisional cathedral was repaired in 1555 and partly reconstructed in 1588. In the meantime, the new cathedral was ideated in the 1550's; Claudio de Arciniega had come from Mexico City to declare the old cathedral unworthy of extensive repairs, and it may be that the plan of the new cathedral was his. (His brother Luis was *maestro mayor* later.) It is certainly closely related to that of Mexico City. For many years it was assumed that a plan by Juan Gómez de Mora, unused in Mexico City, had been utilized in Puebla. This now seems unlikely. Francisco Becerra was *maestro mayor* in 1575, but only materials for construction were assembled at that time. Building proceeded slowly until 1618, when work was halted. Bishop Juan de Palafox y Mendoza vigorously advanced the structure in the 1640's, and it was interiorly completed and dedicated by April 18, 1649. The crossing dome is said to be the earliest true dome in the highland area; it was by Pedro García Ferrer. Like Mexico City, Puebla's cathedral may have been intended to have four towers (one at each corner of the structure), in the manner of Valladolid in Spain. Only two were built, but they are of unusual height (240 feet) because of the solid foundations possible here but difficult in Mexico City. (One tower was not completed until 1768, but they are stylistically similar.) The dimensions of the large, three-aisled interior with chapels are less than those of Mexico City (about 325 feet by 100 feet). Because of its rapid finishing under Palafox and its revision in the Neo-Classical period, it is more uniform in interior appearance than the Cathedral of Mexico.

PUEBLA, REAR VIEW OF CATHEDRAL (pl. 102)

The gray stone cathedral, on the Plaza de la Constitución in Puebla, is somewhat formal and forbidding in appearance—due to its color and the extreme severity of its ornamental detail. Classicist in elements, it nevertheless has the curious medieval-Renaissance elevation and Baroque animation of silhouette with dome and towers which marks most of Mexico's great cathedrals. The building is surrounded by a nineteenth-century cast iron fence, with angelic light standards; this period flavor of Empire classicism with discreet touches of Victorian Rococo perfectly matches the solemn building with its irrepressibly Mexican tile enrichments.

Santo Domingo

The church of Santo Domingo, on the street of the same name, was early associated with the names of Francisco Becerra and Luis de Arciniega. The building was largely completed about 1611. Aside from its magnificent *retablo mayor* of 1688–1690 by Pedro Maldonado and the many other eighteenth-century retables and fittings, the church is known best for the Capilla del Rosario—attached to the left transept. This structure (built after 1632 by Francisco Gutiérrez *et al.*), with its extraordinary stucco decoration and tabernacle (dedicated 1759), was in construction between 1650 and 1690; its inauguration on April 16, 1690, occasioned a book with Fray Diego de Gorozpe's encomiastic description of the "Octava Maravilla del Mundo." The Rosary cult began in Mexico in 1538; it came to Puebla after 1555.

PUEBLA, VAULT DETAIL, CAPILLA DEL ROSARIO, SANTO DOMINGO (pl. 103)

Celebrated as a new wonder or a veritable "Potosí de oro," the elaborate cruciform chapel with a tabernacle crowned in *salomónica tecali* columns seems to be alive with an ecstasy of heavenly joy in the midst of a fantastic ornamental jungle of beige and gold strapwork and foliation in carved stucco. Saints, angelic children, and insignia are engulfed in a waving Saragossa Sea of Mannerist-inspired interlaces (related to Spanish work of the same period, especially in Córdoba). The Pueblan stucco tradition, carried by itinerant workers to Oaxaca, reached a pitch of fervor and craftsmanship here to be attained later only in the small churches near San Francisco Acatepec. (Francisco de la Maza has a full description of the iconography of the Capilla del Rosario in an article in the *Anales del Instituto de Investigaciones Estéticas* of the University of Mexico, Vol. VI, no. 23, pp. 5–29.)

QUERÉTARO (Querétaro)

SAN AGUSTÍN

The church and monastery of the Augustinians, on the corner of the present Calle del Aguila and Calle San Agustín in Querétaro, were constructed in the eighteenth century. The church was opened for use on October 31, 1745, funds having come from Don Julián Díaz de la Pena. Solá suggests that the cloister (1731–1745) was by the Spaniards, Luis Martínez Lucio and Carlos Benito de Butrón Moxica; it would appear, however, that these men supervised construction but may not have provided the design. The cloister foundation was laid about 1748. The monastic buildings and cloister are now the municipal palace of Querétaro.

QUERÉTARO, CLOISTER AND UNFINISHED TOWER, SAN AGUSTÍN (pl. 141)

Various quaint stories have come from the presence of the unusual caryatid and atlantid supports of entablature sections in the first and second levels of this cloister. Some local wags have claimed they represented a deaf and dumb alphabet with their raised hands and splayed legs and feet; if so, the sixteenth-century and seventeenth-century prints which inspired these strange conceits of ornamental architecture, foliage, busts, and limbs, must have come from linguisticians rather than designers! Caryatids and atlantes are almost a Querétaro trademark; they are present on almost every building of the eighteenth century in the town. An interesting variant occurs on the dome of San Agustín; superbly garbed men, with panache feather headdresses (locally thought to be Indian *caciques*, but related to ballet costumes of the French court of Louis XIV) are vigorous elements of the drum of that dome. Similar figures, of which only the lower body was finished, can be seen rimming the top of the uncompleted tower of the church, rising over the undulant cornice of the cloister.

SANTA ROSA DE VITERBO

A convent was founded on this site on Calle de Galván in the seventeenth century. Construction of a chapel, under Don Juan Caballero y Osio began in 1699; after a *real colegio* was established in 1727 (by papal bull in 1732), building proceeded more rapidly. The conventual church was dedicated on January 4, 1752, funds having come from Lieutenant Colonel Don José Velázquez de Lorea. It would seem that the design was by Ignacio Mariano de las Casas, more famous locally for a repeating clock mechanism (now lost) for the church tower. Casas was essentially a mechanical engineer and retable craftsman; and the fabric of the church had to be strengthened by Francisco Gudiño in 1759, with a pair of buttresses which gave the church its principal exterior drama. Francisco Eduardo Tresguerras worked here after 1785, probably revising the tower and enlarging and redecorating the dome area. Tresguerras is responsible for the balustrades; the cloister has the medieval-Mudéjar arches seen in the remarkable house patios of Querétaro and suggests a date earlier than Tresguerras' period. In 1862 the nuns of Santa Rosa were moved to Santa Clara (soon to be closed itself), and the convent of Santa Rosa was converted into a civil hospital—a function it still fulfills, although the church has returned to religious uses.

QUERÉTARO, SIDE ELEVATION OF SANTA ROSA DE VITERBO (pl. 140)

Like all eighteenth-century conventual churches, Santa Rosa had twin portals—here, exceptional Mudéjar-inspired wooden doors surrounded by classicist façades. Aside from its handsome tiled dome and the depressed arches in the cloister, Santa Rosa's principal fame rests today on the photogenic buttresses of the side elevation and the literally fabulous retables, choir screen, pulpit, confessionals, organ case, and sacristy fittings. Closely related in style to the interior of Santa Clara in Querétaro, and more tangentially to the interior of San Agustín at Salamanca (Mexico), the eighteenth-century retables of Santa Rosa are part of a unique group forming the "Querétaro style." Their design and superb realization were the result of an inspired local combination of European and metropolitan Mexican sources, interpreted by designer-craftsmen of exceptional imagination and skill. This school (studied in Baird, "Querétaro Style," *Art Bulletin*, Vol. XXXV [September, 1953]) had connections with designer-craftsmen in the Dolores-

Guanajuato area, and formed a powerful center of regional taste and verve that equaled anything in the large cities of Mexico or Spain.

SAN CRISTÓBAL DE LAS CASAS (Chiapas)

SANTO DOMINGO

The first church of Santo Domingo at San Cristóbal Las Casas was erected between 1528 and 1541; it was replaced by the present structure with a façade of about 1700, and interior fittings of the seventeenth and eighteenth centuries.

SAN CRISTÓBAL LAS CASAS, FAÇADE OF SANTO DOMINGO (pl. 77 and pl. 157, color)

Decisively situated at the head of a flight of stairs and surrounded by an irregular atrium, Santo Domingo at San Cristóbal Las Casas reveals the ornamental influence of Antigua, Guatemala, which, as Kelemen has indicated, was the real cultural capital of this southern outpost of Mexico. The flat, lacelike appliqué of foliation and more abstract patterns on the façade recalls the great Mercedarian church in Antigua. The massing of the façade, with its stubby towers on simple, solid bases in the manner of Oaxaca, emphasizes groups of *salomónicas* for its vertical accentuation. The stepping of the columns forward to frame the rather nondescript niches is an approximation—not of the ornamental niche-pilaster to come, but rather of the powerful vertical buttresses of seventeenth-century Mexican cathedral façades. A close parallel can be seen on the Cathedral of Guadix in Spain, probably later in its execution than Santo Domingo at San Cristóbal.

SAN CRISTÓBAL LAS CASAS, SIDE ELEVATION OF SANTO DOMINGO (pl. 78)

The air of a fortified monastic church of the sixteenth century still clings to this seventeenth-century building. The squared tower buttresses have heavy obeliskoid tops like medieval battlements. The dome, flanked by four small towers in the manner of sentry boxes, is ribbed—symbolically pushing the time back to late medieval forms. Construction is solid and rather low in proportion, reminding one of the frontier character of Chiapas in the later colonial era

when the Mexican highland had become more developed.

SAN CRISTÓBAL LAS CASAS, SIDE PORTAL OF SANTO DOMINGO (pl. 79)

In addition to its almost brutal strength of part, this portal shows the close affiliation of southern Mexico and Guatemala in artistic details. The pilasters at either side of the door combine the "pillow" (so-called because they look like stacked small pillows) pilasters of Guatemala, described by Kelemen, with a *salomónica* half-column. The carving and the ornamental details of the second level, around the center niche, are coarse but visually effective, with herringbone or variants of the chevron pattern on the framing pilasters and bold cascades of spirals and rough foliation at the sides. The general composition is close to the cloister portal of La Merced in Antigua, Guatemala.

SAN CRISTÓBAL LAS CASAS, CHAPEL RETABLE OF SANTO DOMINGO (pl. 80)

There is remarkable homogeneity to the interior decoration of this church. Most of the carved wood paneling, the retables, and other fittings were done in the same style about the same general period. The retables are articulated with Solomonic columns, as one would expect between about 1690 and 1720, when this work was finished. The composition of parts is simple, but the execution is well above average. Half-crowns above the modern pictures of famous virgins on the lower left and right of this retable were rare for the period; they were to be especially developed at Querétaro and Salamanca (Mexico) some sixty or seventy years later in a more complete form. Here there are still touches of Andalusian Spanish influence as well as analogies to Guatemala.

SAN CRISTÓBAL LAS CASAS, DETAIL OF A RETABLE IN SANTO DOMINGO (pl. 81)

This retable, like the base of the pulpit, has a more provincial flavor. The covering of every possible surface with variations of foliate patterns is typically exuberant and naïve. The execution is summary rather than elegant; and the framing of paintings is charmingly out of scale with the decoration. The spiritual affiliation of such work is with Colombia and

Guatemala, rather than Mexico; the date must be about 1700 or slightly earlier. A Santo Niño de Atocha in the central niche is more recent.

SAN CRISTÓBAL LAS CASAS, PULPIT OF SANTO DOMINGO (pl. 82)

The pulpits of the colonial period in Latin America are among the chief adornments of the churches. There are many dazzling examples in Mexico; but among them that of Santo Domingo in San Cristóbal Las Casas is one of the most vivid of the viceregal era. Following the example of the interior walls of this church, which are literally sheathed in carved and gilded wood paneling, the pulpit provides a somewhat more plastically audacious example of the carver's and gilder's art. In the long ramp which leads to the pulpit proper one can see analogies to the sectional paneling and carving of seventeenth and eighteenth century choir stalls—here in richly conceived foliation almost Roman in its authority. The base and canopy of the pulpit are more provincial; a spiky roughness animates these sections, which, like the stone side door of the church, provides a powerful visual effect at some remove. There is bravura but little finesse, and for more exquisite craftsmanship one must turn to the inlaid pulpits of the Bajío area, in north central Mexico.

SAN LUIS DE POTOSÍ (San Luis de Potosí)

CATHEDRAL OF LA EXPECTACIÓN DE LA VIRGEN

Originally a parish church, this church became a cathedral in 1854. The early church on the site (built after 1596) was destroyed in 1670. A new church was begun in 1690, and construction continued into the eighteenth century (1718 is given as a terminal date by some writers, although the dedication was 1737). The interior is principally of the nineteenth century, including the green and white marble and gold tomb of Ignacio Montés de Oca y Obregón, first bishop of Tamaulipas. The side aisles were raised to the level of the nave, and one tower (uncompleted in the eighteenth century) was finished at this time.

SAN LUIS POTOSÍ, FAÇADE OF CATHEDRAL (pl. 134)

Like most of the major churches from here north to Monterrey, this building emphasizes a special variant of the twin-towered eighteenth-century silhouette. The towers are of three stages, forcefully accented with twisted columns earlier in the century and with classical columns later in the century. The façade of the Cathedral of San Luis Potosí is organized around two salient, canted wall sections, reminding one slightly of La Soledad at Oaxaca (pl. 83); but here the projecting sections with Solomonic half-columns and classicist pilasters framing the niches are dominated by the towers, rather than vice versa. (Its inspiration probably came from de Arrieta's façade for the Guadalupe Basilica.) The tabernacle over the center of the façade would appear to be Neo-Classical. Notable in San Luis Potosí is the handsome brownish stone. The cathedral (on the east side of Plaza Hidalgo) is a duskier variant of Saltillo, Durango, and Monterrey, and, like Zacatecas, which is stylistically very different but of a similar color, seems to be more substantial because of its tone.

EL CARMEN

Begun in 1603, the present building dates from 1749 (some writers give 1732) to 1764 and was built with funds provided by the Sevillian Nicolás F. Torres. The building faces the small Plaza de Morelos.

SAN LUIS POTOSÍ, UPPER CENTER, FAÇADE OF EL CARMEN (pl. 135)

One of the most daringly original façades of the eighteenth century, the front of El Carmen has the winsome extravagance of obviously local talent. Solomonic columns (in the first level) and *estípites* (in the second) are suspended against a setting which is conceived in theatrical terms, having massed drapery, like theater curtains, carved at the top and sides to "reveal" the lively composition of architectural sculpture and ornament. The *estípites* in the second level are classic examples of their form— hard, almost metallic in contour, and covered with ornamental sculpture that combines foliation in the Renaissance-Baroque tradition and mannered *pinjantes*. An obvious disinterest in traditional architectural distinction of parts, whether tectonic or not, is apparent in the arch of foliation which surrounds the window and its *estípites*, breaking up into the entablature above. Even a kind of Neo-Gothic is suggested here in the ogival shape of the foliate arch.

SAN LUIS POTOSÍ, LOWER CENTER, FAÇADE OF EL CAR-
     MEN (pl. 136)

Unusual on this first level are the *salomónicas* im-
prisoned in vertical strips of carving. This type, seen
on a few other northern Mexican buildings, suggests
an Oriental parallel in the Chinese carved ivory balls
within balls; certainly the inspiration came from
some more delicate material than stone. Elaborately
interlaced cords, reminiscent of Leonardo da Vinci's
knot patterns but probably derived from the tassels
of a cardinal's hat, occupy the space over the niches;
and more woven influences appear in the plaited
patterns on the cylindrical bases of the *salomónicas*
and the smaller knot patterns of the pilasters framing the door proper. The strapwork-decorated pedestals of the twisted columns, the very "indigenous"
cherub heads here and there, and the almost frenzied
profusion of foliation in the frieze create an ensemble
that is international in source but entirely local in
conception, and especially in craftsmanship. Particularly fascinating are the plungerlike decorations of
the arch over the door, similar to those of the side
portal of El Carmen, and to ornaments over the door
of San Diego, Guanajuato. They are Manueline in
origin but made half-Mudéjar and half-Rococo here.

SAN LUIS POTOSÍ, WOODEN DOOR, FAÇADE OF EL CARMEN
     (pl. 137)

One can only marvel at the infinite permutations
and combinations possible with a few Mudéjar-inspired geometric patterns on the eighteenth-century
wooden doors. Dating this work more exactly to the
period after 1765 or 1770 are the *rocaille* fragments
of some panels, combined with foliation and flower
garlands.

SAN LUIS POTOSÍ, "PROSCENIUM" RETABLE, LEFT TRAN-
     SEPT OF EL CARMEN (pl. 138)

If the façade of El Carmen chatters in many lan-
guages of ornament, but with a distinctly local accent,
this incredible triumph of the retable designer stut-
ters with an almost hysterical brilliance. Executed in
the comparatively rare material of *argamasa* (a kind
of cement), like the other wall retables at El Carmen, this white (now gray), tan, and gold composition is a particularly good example of the anti-

structural trends of the later eighteenth century.
There are *estípites*, but they flank strongly salient
ornamental niche-pilasters, so that the *estípites* are
reduced to a lesser role. The upper center of this
retable moves forward in a reduplication of flat surfaces that is dizzying. Yet the composition is superbly
integrated, and shows a much more consistent use of
progressive Mexico City trends than does the façade.
The influence of Lorenzo Rodríguez' Sagrario façades (pl. 95) is basic here, but this is the logical
extension of the still firm structural order of those
façades into the delirium of late Baroque rhythmic
repetition and Rococo glitter. The date must be about
1775. The transept retables at La Valenciana show
the same manifestations of the circle of Rodríguez,
expanding to the limits of the technique in these rich
northern towns. Beyond the entrance in the lower
center of this towering retable (one might call it a
"proscenium" retable, as it frames a stagelike space)
is a beautiful chapel or *camarín* badly burned in
1957 and now being repaired. Other *argamasa* and
wooden collateral retables remain, but the interior of
the church has been extensively reworked in the
nineteenth and twentieth century.

CHAPEL OF NUESTRA SEÑORA DE ARANZAZÚ

Cults centering around the Basque protectress, the
Virgin of Aranzazú, were especially developed by
the Franciscans of northern Mexico in the eighteenth
century (compare the Aranzazú chapel near San
Francisco, Guadalajara). The building in San Luis
Potosí seems to have been begun about 1700, but
was largely decorated about 1760–1780.

SAN LUIS POTOSÍ, ENTRANCE FAÇADE, ARANZAZÚ CHAPEL
     (pl. 139)

An interesting comparison with the transept or "proscenium" retable of El Carmen can be made here.
Although carved in stone rather than *argamasa*, this
façade has the delicacy of stucco work. It is stylistically a little earlier than the Carmen retables. The
estípites are reduplicated, but they are still the main
articulating elements. The mixtilinear arch over the
door (in the manner of Rodríguez) does not lead on
into a group of stepped and spiraled ornamental
parts which break down traditional horizontal order,
as they do at El Carmen's transept retable. The com-

position is meticulously thought out, elegantly executed, and of a delicacy rare in northern Mexico. Inside, this decorum is rudely shattered by a brilliantly polychromatic décor that would appear to be twentieth century in some color details (at least the color has been heightened in the twentieth century), although the motifs and ornamental planning are eighteenth century. The execution is crude, but the white vaults with red, green, and gold tracery, the cerise, gray and green walls, and the malachite green dome over cerise pendentives trumpet a challenge to the eye which the inconspicuous street entrance of this chapel-church, and the serene portal at the head of the stair from the street, would never suggest. A rose stone *estípite retablo mayor* inside is echoed in wall pilasters in the form of *estípites*.

SAN MIGUEL DE ALLENDE (Guanajuato)

SAN FRANCISCO

Originally San Antonio, the present church of San Francisco in San Miguel Allende was begun on June 29, 1779, and finished on April 13, 1799. By some writers, the tower is attributed to Tresguerras.

SAN MIGUEL ALLENDE, REAR VIEW OF SAN FRANCISCO (pl. 143)

Seen from the little plaza or atrium in front of the Oratory of San Felipe Neri, the back of San Francisco has an almost sixteenth-century starkness, with its massive pier buttresses. Of course, the high dome and the tower as well as a plan with squared apse and fairly deep transepts mark it as of the eighteenth century. More than the parish church of San Miguel —which is a hybrid of Neo-Classical and Neo-Gothic —the monumental simplicity and scenographic effectiveness of San Francisco dominate the lower reaches of the town and especially the market streets with their white planes of umbrellas slicing into the sun.

SAN MIGUEL ALLENDE, DETAIL, FAÇADE OF SAN FRANCISCO (pl. 144)

Attributed some years ago by Dr. Atl (Gerardo Murillo) to Lorenzo Rodríguez (who died in 1774, five years before this church was begun), this painted, rose stone façade is—as Angulo has written—little

inferior to Rodríguez' known works, at least in execution. In conception it is rather delicate (like Tepotzotlán's façade) and suffers from diffusion of its *estípite* accents over a rather wide surface. Obviously, it is by someone from Rodríguez' circle, who has chosen to minimize the structural character of the Sagrario façades and emphasize the nontectonic qualities. Being at least twenty or twenty-five years later than the Sagrario façades, this façade is closer to the triumph of the ornamental niche-pilaster over the *estípite* in the 1780's. Still, the *estípites* are more dominant here than on La Valenciana, finished in 1788; of the Guanajuato churches, San Felipe (the former Jesuit church, La Compañía) bears the closest analogies to San Francisco in San Miguel. The stained glass window is more recent.

CHURCH OF THE THIRD ORDER OF ST. FRANCIS

The Tercer Orden de San Francisco (founded originally for lay members who wished to assume some of the austerities of friars and nuns) often had a church near the major buildings of the Franciscans in Mexican towns. The Third Order at San Miguel was opened on July 28, 1713, with funds in part from Don Manuel Urtusautegui's will of January 3, 1709.

SAN MIGUEL ALLENDE, FAÇADE, EL TERCER ORDEN (pl. 145)

The unassuming little façade of the Third Order, at one side of the plaza in front of San Francisco, is a perfect example of a modest type common in Mexico. It could almost be the archetype of hundreds of similar façades, going back to a composition first used in the sixteenth century. The arched door, with window above and niche above that, is framed with pilasters—as are window and niche. The types of vertical accents may change, but a fairly regular classicist form is by no means uncommon in the otherwise anticlassical age of the *salomónica*, *estípite*, and ornamental niche-pilaster. A few elements of transition from the Baroque (broken pedimental sections) persist; the staging of parts from wide to narrow, however, goes back to the pre-Baroque, probably to Islamic-inspired origins of this façade composition, generally more common on side portals in Mexico. The Mudéjar-inspired wooden door is, invariably, present. A *campanario*, combined here with an *espadaña* (that is, a small bell tower combined with a wall belfry), animates the top of the building, but the wall surfaces are undecorated. As in the other churches of San Miguel, it is the pink stone which confers its own felicity on this stereotyped but endlessly useful façade composition.

ORATORY (EL ORATORIO DE SAN FELIPE NERI)

The oratory church occupies the site of a chapel for the mulattos, originally dedicated to Christ Presented to the People. After a particularly affecting Easter sermon by a curate of Pátzcuaro, Juan Antonio Pérez de Espinosa, the curate was prevailed upon to found a Filippine oratory in San Miguel. The church was finished about 1714. An important addition was the chapel of the Santa Casa de Loreto, founded in 1736 with funds from Don Manuel Tomás de la Canal (36,000 pesos).

SAN MIGUEL ALLENDE, FAÇADE, EL ORATORIO (pl. 142)

The stone of the area, varying from ashes of roses to brown, has been given a coat of pink paint here to make it more uniform (Angulo calls the façade *argamasa* for this reason). The façade is clearly and harmoniously composed in the simple, traditional façade and retable design of four vertical accents, with arched door in the first level and window above (and a framed niche in the third level). Although the columns are not really *salomónicas*, the designer has cleverly simulated those forms with a band of flat, carved leaves around a cylinder. These very pleasing columns with their unarchitectural but effective tiered scales (like bark or a palm tree's crown) are a tranquil repetition of foliated columns common in northern Mexico (the cathedral of Zacatecas has more aggressive variants). The fairly complete investiture of all the other surfaces of the façade with flat foliation is surprisingly unobtrusive. Of course, the effective setting of the Oratory, on a little atrium above the market streets of San Miguel, and the fine cypresses that frame its façade from a distance, confer a special aura on this agreeable local piece of theater. San José, San Juan Bautista, San Felipe, San Pedro, and San Pablo are the *dramatis personae* of the façade.

TAXCO OR TASCO (Guerrero)

PARISH CHURCH (LA PARROQUIA DE SANTA PRISCA Y SAN SEBASTIÁN)

A church dedicated to Santa Prisca, in Taxco, was founded in the sixteenth century. There was work in 1634–1637 and again in 1728, but the present church is essentially the creation of a special, active building period between 1751 and 1758. At the behest and expense of the immensely wealthy mining magnate, José de la Borda (who had in 1748 discovered a rich vein of silver ore), Diego Durán Berruecos—a Spaniard, registered in a census of 1753 in Mexico City—designed and supervised construction of a superb new church dedicated to Santa Prisca and San Sebastián. Durán Berruecos was aided by Juan Caballero. Work was completed on December 3, 1758, and the church was dedicated on May 11–12, 1759. De la Borda had in the meantime temporarily lost his fortune and had been forced to sell to the Cathedral of Mexico certain precious ecclesiastic objects intended for Santa Prisca. He soon made a new discovery of ore and again became one of the richest men of his time. The retables in the church are of two distinctly different periods of fashion. Those in the apse and transepts probably were begun in the last phases of construction on the church during the first bonanza; those in the nave date from some fifteen or twenty years later and represent new bonanza gifts to various saints.

TAXCO, GENERAL VIEW OF SANTA PRISCA (pl. 117)

Situated, like Guanajuato and Zacatecas, on the sides of steeply inclined hills, Taxco is the classic south central Mexican mining community of the eighteenth century. Although it has received a modern bonanza of tourism, based partly on its attractive setting and partly on a revival of silver-making, the configuration of low, tiled roofs building to a climax in the parish church is almost unchanged from the late Baroque period. The richly decorated church tower tops on virtually unornamented bases suggest to Kubler the lofty towers of Ecija in Spain. They would seem more likely to be special developments, in the mid-eighteenth century and later, of towers with simple bases and ornamented tops which had been current in Mexico since the later sixteenth century, although their proportions are almost those of the very tall, slender Islamic-inspired towers of southern Spain. In any event, these needle-sharp late Baroque "minarets" provide the usual crisp punctuation of the later viceregal parish churches and especially of pilgrimage churches (cf. Tepalcingo). The masterful dome, with its brilliant tiled surface and inscription—"Glory to God in the Highest"—adds the inevitable "period" after the arrestingly conceived "colon" of the towers. The balustrade with ornaments on pedestals further accentuates the skyline of the church, and large, handsomely framed windows in the upper level of the sides open the interior outwards to an expansive—if simple—interpenetration of light. The side door, and a remarkable period homogeneity of atrium wall, iron work, and church proper, complete a composition that is virtually unique for the consistency and cohesiveness of its design. Only the Santuario de Ocotlán, above Tlaxcala, has the same exterior effect of dominating a hill setting; its atrium has been rewalled and reworked more recently to ensure its unity with the church. (Kelemen, *Baroque and Rococo in Latin America*, pp. 81–82 and pl. 35, describes and illustrates this superb building. A master's essay by Mary Elizabeth Smith, "Two Non-Metropolitan Examples of the Late Eighteenth-Century *Retablo*-Façade in Mexico," for Columbia University, New York, June, 1960, discusses the symbolism of the façade at Ocotlán.) However, both Santa Prisca at Taxco and the Santuario de Ocotlán gain much of their ultimate drama from the contrast of fabric color and the theatrical cloud and sky effects of these mountain regions. At Taxco the church is ashes of roses throughout with the polychromatic yellow, blue, and white of the dome tiles for variety. At Ocotlán the white plastered stone façade and tower tops contrast with orange-red "lizard-skin" tiled tower bases.

TAXCO, RELIEF, UPPER CENTER, FAÇADE OF SANTA PRISCA (pl. 118)

The façade of Santa Prisca at Taxco is probably the most sophisticated work in Mexico of its period, and reflects the conservative and progressive trends of Andalucía of the mid-century. Slightly earlier in general stylistic evolution than the Sagrario façades in Mexico City, which are its only rivals for progres-

sivism, the façade at Taxco shows a persisting enthusiasm for the *salomónica* which relates it to Granadine and Sevillian work of the earlier eighteenth century (Hurtado and Figueroa especially come to mind). Yet its decisive support of the ornamental niche-pilaster, pushing forward aggressively between the Corinthian columns in the first level, and less vigorously continued in the second level, is even more apparent than in Rodríguez' Sagrario façades (pl. 95 illustrates the south façade of the Sagrario). The only *estípites* on this building are the corner pilasters of the towers. The ornamental language is a rich purée of Baroque, mannered and almost Rococo, spiced with classicism and Mudéjar geometry. The end result, however, is somehow more Spanish than Mexican in the façade proper. It is interesting that Rodríguez would declare himself more ardently for Mexicanism than Durán Berruecos. Divorced from its towers and dome, this façade could grace any major religious or secular building in Andalucía of its time. The relief of the Baptism of Christ, in its lavish frame, is more Mexican in conception and execution and suggests both the charm and the lack of sophistication in this rich but nonmetropolitan mining town. It is revealing that, throughout the eighteenth century in Mexico, the ornamental sculptors are far less easy to classify as "provincial" and "metropolitan." They quickly mastered the subtlest nuances of new fashions—as here. The figure sculptors persisted in revealing their lack of training on a wide, international scene; while their work is often agreeable or technically adequate, it is distinctly local.

TAXCO, SIDE PORTAL OF SANTA PRISCA (pl. 119)

The powerfully plastic side portal of Santa Prisca is a perfect postscript to the main façade. Here, framing the paneled wooden doors, are the ornamental pilasters, which on the main façade are still flanked by classicist or Solomonic columns. Now these deeply carved pseudo pilasters are alone. Although the broken pediment and the rusticated friezes suggest typical mid-century Mexican adaptations of Andalusian forms, the reliefs and figure sculpture again convey a naïveté which is closer to the hearts of the parishioners here. The often inspired deshabille of such a convenient "check stand" as the iron cross on a stone pedestal at the left of the door is an important part of the Mexican aesthetic. Its casual configurations of baskets, *rebozos,* and people create the special overtones that distinguish Mexican life, and by extension Mexican art, from the formalism of Spanish life and art. To view Santa Prisca as a superb reliquary of a rich man would be false; it is a superb reliquary, executed in part in Spanish, and in part in Mexican, taste. But its total meaning is bound up with the daily life of Taxco, whether in the eighteenth or the twentieth century. It is as much a matter of odor and "local color" (as much as that phrase has been overused) as of magnificently carved rose stone and a dazzling sequence of retables.

TAXCO, *retablo mayor* OF SANTA PRISCA (pl. 120)

The retables of Santa Prisca are of two different eras of fashion. Those in the apse and transept form a group related to the nave retables at San Martín in Tepotzotlán and appear to be by Isidoro Vicente de Balbás (son of Gerónimo Balbás?). They were probably executed about 1755. Like the nave retables at Tepotzotlán, they begin to reveal an excessive fussiness of detail, an almost repellent elaboration. There is a moment, especially among certain designers, when the fantasy and bravura of such works as the apse and transept retables at Taxco draw perilously close to a lack of coördination. One must have drunk deep of the heady mixtures of the period to see the distinction. The *retablo mayor* of Santa Prisca is spastic rather than rhythmic; its *estípites* and ornamental niche-pilasters are consumed with a terrible surface agitation. A few years later, as in the Carmen at San Luis Potosí, this same hysterical agitation will be reorganized and made more understandable, even if less structural. Indeed, at Santa Prisca itself, the nave retables (*ca.* 1770 or 1775) are more attractive and more completely nontectonic. Still, the ultimate effect here is a marvel of gilded surfaces, which enhances the total verve of an extraordinary interior.

TECAMACHALCO (Puebla)

FRANCISCAN MONASTERY OF LA ASUNCIÓN DE NUESTRA SEÑORA

A community was established at this site in 1543. The church, dedicated in 1551, was completed in 1557, although the adjacent monastery was not finished until about 1585. The church façade has a tower with an inscription in Spanish and Nahuatl which gives its inception date as 1589 and its completion date as 1591. On the underside of the church choir there are important frescoes by Juan Gerson of 1561–1562. The buildings are in a semi-ruined state today.

TECAMACHALCO, GENERAL VIEW OF FRANCISCAN CHURCH (pl. 16)

Although of great simplicity, the façade of the Franciscan monastic church at Tecamachalco, is a tour de force of proportion and carefully planned ornamental parts. The original façade, without the tower, would have been distinguished for its fine handling of the mixtilinear arch over the doors and the slightly unusual *alfiz* above (instead of being rectilinear, it has curved corners). Even the window with its ogival decorated arch is a refined, if unelaborate, repetition in variation of the more complex arch below. With the addition of the tower to the left of this façade, the starkly strong crenelation over the façade was more effectively developed into a part of the total design—now echoed in the crenelation of the tower.

TEPALCINGO (Morelos)

PILGRIMAGE CHURCH (EL SANTUARIO DE JESÚS NAZARENO)

The cult was founded in Tepalcingo in the seventeenth century. An older church, still standing, was the seat of this pilgrimage devotional center until 1782. The very unusual present church dates from 1759 to 1782 (dated by an inscription on a painting under the *coro*). The building was licensed on February 19, 1758, through the aid of Don José de Asso y Otal. Among the *mayordomos* from 1758 to 1785 were Juan Francisco de Hurtoza, José Salvido y Goitia, Juan José de Ubilla, and Nicolás Icazbalceta.

TEPALCINGO, UPPER SECTION, FAÇADE, EL SANTUARIO (pl. 110)

Constantino Reyes Valerio has published a full description of this most unusual folk-oriented façade. It is related to a group of churches in the area, including Santa María Jolalpan, San Lucas Tzicatlán and Santa María Tlancualpicán. The churches of

Jesús Nazareno Tepalcingo and Santa María Jolalpan are especially close in idea and execution of their façades. Reyes Valerio explains the presence of this richly decorated local masterpiece in terms both of the importance of the saint and the assistance of wealthy local hacienda owners. Certainly the Santuario at Tepalcingo is one of the great expressions of completely provincial Mexican taste which rise to the level of the Calvaries of Brittany or some of the Romanesque churches of France and Spain. Its iconography is complex, and includes references to the Passion, to Christian history and doctrine, and to divine mercy. The ornamental details, at once suggesting Celtic, Islamic, and Baroque analogies, are essentially western European; it is their execution which conjures up Oriental, barbaric, and primitive associations.

TEPALCINGO, DETAIL, RIGHT LOWER SIDE OF FAÇADE, EL SANTUARIO (pl. 111)

Among the most important figures in this section of the façade are: the Christ Bound and Mocked in the upper niche; St. Peter in the lower niche; Eve reclining in the frieze of the pilaster beside the door opening. The rough technical execution of the figure sculpture and many of the poses recall Romanesque and Gothic sources. The indecisive alternation between plastic and planar is typical of the unsophisticated artisan; yet, rather than being merely grotesque and quaint (which it certainly is in some measure), this façade becomes a deeply moving folk drama, with the *personae* of a Christian history which verges often on atavistic pantheism, investing not only Christ and his forebears and followers but all of nature. Some of the ornamental areas seem almost Polynesian, and the delicate repeats on the right recall Near Eastern and North African developments out of the Roman era. This is not so far from the truth. Tepalcingo represents the residual pattern sense of all great primitive art and the free interpretation of classical forms which created much of the greatest medieval art.

TEPALCINGO, EVE, FROM RIGHT SIDE OF DOOR AREA, FAÇADE, EL SANTUARIO (pl. 112)

Reyes Valerio makes a number of telling comparisons between the sculpture of Tepalcingo and the monuments of Romanesque France. The Eve is particularly close to the famous Eve of Autun, while the Evangelist on the column, above and to the right of Eve, is related to early Romanesque sculpture at Saint Benoit-sur-Loire or Saint Mesme-de-Chinon in France. The hideous grotesque masks (of a kind of devil below the Evangelist and of a frog above) are full of the nightmarish aspects of medieval symbols of the powers of darkness, or the possession of natural things with diabolical force.

TEPEACA (Puebla)

FRANCISCAN MONASTERY OF SAN FRANCISCO

The great Franciscan monastic complex at Tepeaca dates from the 1540's, although work continued into the 1550's and was not entirely finished until the later sixteenth century, with some phases continuing as late as 1778.

TEPEACA, SIDE PORTAL, EL TERCER ORDEN (pl. 114)

As at Cuernavaca and elsewhere, the Third Order here had a smaller church near the great monastic church of the Franciscans. Like that of Cuernavaca, its construction appears to date largely from the eighteenth century. Certainly this side portal is not earlier than 1700, and possibly is as late as 1735 or 1740. The twisted columns, and the broken cornice sections above each column, are Late Baroque. The curious gable with its stepped moldings on the surface suggests the animated silhouette of the mid-eighteenth century. The figure sculpture, in relief or in the round, is undistinguished in intrinsic quality, as is the ornamental sculpture; and yet the *conjunto* (the ensemble—a very important word for Mexico) is full of *chiaroscuro* potential and vivacious movement. It does not rise to the level of inspired primitivism like Tepalcingo (pl. 110), but it does reveal that fairly routine projects could have a local distinction in the eighteenth century as in the sixteenth.

TEPOSCOLULA (Oaxaca)

DOMINICAN MONASTERY OF SAN PEDRO Y SAN PABLO

Originally a secular settlement, Teposcolula was occupied by the Dominicans following difficulties at

Yanhuitlán with the *encomendero*. Under their early director, Fray Juan Cabrera, the friars built a church in the 1550's. The present complex dates from a slightly later period, when buildings were constructed on a better hillside site nearby. Work was still continuing on the new church and buildings in the 1570's, and some features are even later.

TEPOSCOLULA, OPEN CHAPEL OF DOMINICAN CHURCH (pl. 42)

The open chapel at Teposcolula is one of the most elaborate of the sixteenth century in Mexico. It is closely related to the open chapel at Coixtlahuaca in this area. Double naves with a beautiful Renaissance arcade in the middle spread laterally from an hexagonal space covered with rib vaulting. The naves originally had wooden roofs, and raised sections at the ends away from the hexagon. Buttresses with paneled surfaces lead the eye into the center of this richly ordered, classicist-detailed design. Kubler dates it to the 1570's, after Coixtlahuaca.

TEPOSCOLULA, DETAIL, LOWER RIGHT CENTER, FAÇADE OF DOMINICAN CHURCH (pl. 43)

Simple half-columns on this façade flank figure niches with various saints in very high relief (giving the appearance of being in the round). As in so much early colonial sculpture, there is an untutored technical crudeness about these figures and their carved supports which is paralleled later in the colonial era by local sculptors with the same lack of training and finesse. One must, however, go beyond this seeming ineptitude to experience the pleasure of a devotional art that is oriented to more than craftsmanly virtues. The truculent angelic figure supporting the saint's pedestal is especially delightful in this respect.

TEPOSCOLULA, DOOR TO CHAPEL OF SANTA GERTRUDIS (pl. 44)

It is impossible to date these wooden Mudéjar-inspired doors accurately. Most of the more elaborately paneled examples seem to have been executed in the eighteenth century; those of the sixteenth century were simpler and depended often on nail patterns rather than geometric recessed paneling. Certainly the configuration of parts of this particular example suggests a Baroque composition moving into the Rococo. Aside from the date, however, the important factor here is the *conjunto*—the casual poetry dear to Mexican aesthetics (and hardly so intentional) of a fine heavy arch on stubby columns with quasi-Romanesque capitals; the painting of the arch (repainting in the manner of the sixteenth century); the stone floor with its irregular pattern of fitted parts; and the special atmosphere and quality of light which comes into the cool old building from the dusty outside.

TEPOSCOLULA, INTERIOR OF CHAPEL OF SANTA GERTRUDIS (pl. 45)

One could almost imagine oneself in some Russian or Romanesque crypt in this chamber. The low proportions of the arches, the massive ribs, and especially the superb authority of the great but low twisted column suggest the beginning stages of Mont Saint Michel or a set for Ivan the Terrible. A few *santos*, paintings, and the passing sparkle of a cut paper enrichment on one of the arches bring the country and its religion more clearly into focus; and a close inspection of the tiled floor reveals that it must be related to the Mediterranean rather than to the coast of Brittany or the Black Sea. At Easter an image of El Señor de la Caña is venerated on the chapel altar here.

TEPOTZOTLÁN OR TEPOZOTLÁN (México)

SAN MARTÍN

The Seminario de San Martín was founded by the Jesuits at Tepotzotlán in 1584. (The *convento* had been established in 1582; the *noviciado* dates from 1586, and the *colegio* from 1606.) A cornerstone for the present church was laid on May 27, 1670, and the building was completed in 1682. The façade was not conceived and built until 1760–1762. Interior fittings and retables are of the utmost importance for eighteenth-century Mexico, and are remarkably well preserved—virtually *in toto*. The magnificent apse and transept retables are by a different hand than the somewhat fussy nave retables; the latter compare with the apse and transept retables at Taxco, and are probably by Isidoro Vicente Balbás. Tepotzotlán was abandoned by the Jesuits when they were expelled from Mexico and other parts of the Hispanic realm in

1767. The seminary is maintained as a national monument today.

TEPOTZOTLÁN, UPPER CENTER OF FAÇADE AND TOWER, SAN MARTÍN (pl. 99)

After many years of uncertainty as to who might have been the architect of this façade, it is still problematic on documentary evidence. The name on a dated metal plaque (1762) on the rear of the façade seems to be merely that of the artisan who carved the plaque (Francisco Juan Morales). This façade is a crucial example of the *estípite* era. It is later in date and later in idea than Lorenzo Rodríguez' Sagrario façades, with which it has often been connected; and it is superior in quality to the façade of La Santísima Trinidad in Mexico City, sometimes also attributed to Rodríguez, but inferior to his work and possibly by Iniesta, who was working at Santísima in 1781. San Martín's façade has an exquisite refinement of detail and high quality of execution that make it part of the metropolitan Mexico City group of the developed *estípite* type, which gradually submitted to the nontectonic enthusiasms of the end of the eighteenth century. The best descriptions are in Valle's monograph, and in de la Maza, "Tepotzotlán," *Cuadernos Medicos* (September, 1954), p. 37. Only one staged tower was completed; and the upper part of the façade (seen from the rear) is clearly distinct in construction from the lower part.

TEPOTZOTLÁN, VIEW TO *camarín* AND REAR OF FAÇADE OF SAN MARTÍN (pl. 100)

Some confusion about the construction of this *camarín* is based on the proliferation of chapels of a special type in this area of the seminary. The chapel of the Santa Casa de Loreto and its *camarín* is usually dated 1679–1680. The chapel of San José was dedicated on April (May?) 27, 1738. Wilder Weismann dates the stucco decorations of the *camarín* to the seventeenth century, and the *estípite* retables to the later 1730's. While a tradition for polychromatic stucco was certainly present in the seventeenth century, the telescoping lantern of this *camarín* (interior in pl. 162, color)—above the banded vault in the manner of the mihrab at the mosque of Corboda—is unusually spatial for 1680. Such a combination of banded vaults and a gradually telescoping or constricted layering of light source from above was not importantly developed in Italy until the later seventeenth century; it is unlikely that it would appear so early in Mexico unless Father Zappa (who initiated the Loreto cult in 1680) had been in contact with Guarini in Torino. It is possible that vault decorations and retables were executed together about 1740 to 1750; perhaps the entire structure was reworked after 1738, using the lower walls of an earlier *camarín*.

TEPOZTLÁN (Morelos)

DOMINICAN MONASTERY OF LA NATIVIDAD DE NUESTRA SEÑORA

Founded by 1559, the Dominican house at Tepoztlán has a *convento* of 1580 and a church that was completed in 1588. At the base of towering mountains not far from Cuernavaca, where there had been an important pre-Conquest shrine, Tepoztlán has profited from its isolation to retain much of its sixteenth-century flavor. The church is not richly endowed interiorly, but the cloister is fine and the views from parts of the *convento* show the astute planning which preceded the site selection of these early monasteries.

TEPOZTLÁN, FAÇADE OF DOMINICAN CHURCH (pl. 40)

Kubler suggests a number of comparisons for this metallically sharp façade, including the side door of the Dominican monastic church at Coixtlahuaca and the side door of the Franciscan monastic church at Tlalnepantla, both of which are of the same relatively small scale and have obvious classicist features like Tepoztlán. Kubler, Neumeyer, and Wilder Weismann all link the sculpture here to Calpan and Huaquechula, although it is (as Wilder Weismann points out) really of two different styles: that below the pediment is flat and purely ornamental, and that above is plastic and figural. Wilder Weismann suggests that the lower part may have been ideated by Francisco Becerra, who left Mexico before the church was built. The iconography of the upper part includes the Virgin of the Immaculate Conception (and yet she holds the child), flanked by Santo Domingo de Guzmán and Santa Catarina de Siena.

Below are the Dominican crosses of Alcántara, monograms of María, and the sun and moon. Despite the somewhat mixed stylistic character of the façade, it does have an irrational rationale from the tiny angels supporting the half-columns, on the extreme left and right of the portal, to the large angels with the plaque above. What few have mentioned is that the pedimented portal area is nothing more than a flattened *posa*, and the presence of the pediment is therefore quite logical, as part of the original design.

TEPOZTLÁN, *posa* (pl. 41)

The ribbed vaults with tiercerons of the *posa* at Tepoztlán make this small oratory seem more impressive than its size would imply. (Only one *posa* is well preserved.) The exterior design is of the simplest—shell-headed niches at the corners and a large, semi-circular arched entrance with quasi-Ionic half-columns supporting the arch. Crosses of Alcántara decorate the columns below the capital. Among the striking presences at Tepoztlán, of a nonarchitectural but relevant nature, are the beetling mountains which rise above the atrium and link the Dominican oratories with the Indian oratories high overhead.

TLACOCHAHUAYA (Oaxaca)

Dominican Monastery of Santo Domingo

The Dominican establishment at Tlacochahuaya, south of Oaxaca, dates from the sixteenth century. The atrium and cloister of the present complex date apparently from that period. The church was rebuilt in the seventeenth and possibly the eighteenth century; at least there was extensive redecoration well into the later eighteenth century.

TLACOCHAHUAYA, GENERAL VIEW OF DOMINICAN CHURCH AND MONASTERY (pl. 67)

The low atrium wall makes a token gesture to defensiveness with its widely spaced merlons turning into obelisks. The classicist atrium doorway rises into a very simple Baroque upper part, animated with more obelisk-crowned finials. Behind is the church, with a façade which is stylistically of the later seventeenth century and is related to the Cathedral of San Cristóbal Las Casas. Everywhere in this forecourt

and façade area there is a spareness and classicist sobriety of detail which accords with the massive, earthquake-country construction of walls and towers. The dazzling interior of the church comes with the same surprise as at Santo Domingo, Oaxaca, where the entrance elements are equally severe (pl. 59).

TLACOCHAHUAYA, ATRIUM PORTAL (pl. 68)

Seen from the atrium side, this entrance door has an even more Baroque appearance. The classicist pilasters on the outer face are eliminated on this face, and a simple, deep space with shell-like covering leads the eye to a delicately scrolled iron grill and pair of doors—based on eighteenth-century forms but probably more recent. There is an almost North African austerity in the intense white stuccoed gate and its shaded recess.

TLACOCHAHUAYA, *posa* (pl. 69)

The atrium oratories or *capillas posas* at Tlacochahuaya are entirely different from the more elaborately decorated *posas* of central Mexico. Here in the south, following a Dominican preference for the severe Mannerist classicism of the Herreran phase of later sixteenth-century architecture, exterior details are starkly plain. The *posa* arches rise from corbels at the sides and meet at a massive squared pier with a suggestion of the Tuscan order in its moldings. Rather than being free-standing as they often are in central Mexico, the *posas* here are an integral part of the atrium wall, and part of its solid strength.

TLACOCHAHUAYA, CHURCH INTERIOR TOWARD *retablo mayor* (pl. 70)

It is difficult to date the decoration of the interior of Santo Domingo exactly, pending more definite documentary evidence. The *retablo mayor* appears to be of the later seventeenth century, as do the retables framing the apse. However, the tabernacles in the lower center of each of these retables must be not earlier than 1770, with their *rocaille* patterns, mixtilinear cornices, and ornamental corner pilasters. Though the painting in the retables proper is undistinguished, it is related especially to trends of the eighteenth century; it is conceivable that the retables were reworked in part toward the end of the century. The wonderfully colored fresco painting of the vaults is certainly eighteenth-century, too, with its numerous Dominican roses and religious panels.

TLACOCHAHUAYA, PULPIT (pl. 71)

There is a mannered, almost metallic quality to the carving and ornament of this pulpit. Stylistically it is closer to 1700 than 1750 or 1770, and again one feels the folkloristic character of eastern Europe clinging to this remote Mexican church. The "illumination" of a naked electric light bulb was undreamed of in the later colonial era, but it is really no more out of character here than the trumpeting figure in the tabernacle of the canopy, with his own special variant of holy "illumination." Behind the pulpit, a painted retable in the transept carries on the unsophisticated, delightful illusionism of the vaults, with their flowers in place of the actual illusionism of the sixteenth-century coffering (as in the refectory at Actopan).

TLACOCHAHUAYA, CHURCH VAULT DETAIL (FRESCO) (pl. 72)

In place of the rich investiture of stucco ornament, painted and gilded, that makes the Dominican churches of Puebla and Oaxaca so vibrant from within, the somewhat more isolated and less grand church of Santo Domingo at Tlacochahuaya must be content with painting. Like Tlacolula, not far away, Tlacochahuaya depends for its over-all impression on these decorative enrichments of the walls and vaults; but the execution here is somewhat more light-hearted than at Tlacolula, and somewhat less technically serious. The Holy Trinity in the present detail, while iconographically adequate, is altogether more festive than dogmatic. The painter has representation problems with Christ's right hand and knee, but the jocund cherubs below more than obviate these slight difficulties; they make the scene a friendly convivium, and the Dove above fairly radiates happiness on the gently aged God the Father and graceful Christ.

TLACOCHAHUAYA, BAPTISTRY DOORWAY (pl. 73)

For all of its ornamental relationships to the source-books of the Renaissance and southern Baroque, and its essentially light, eighteenth-century color scheme, the painted frames of paintings and arch, of vault lines and surfaces, inescapably brings to mind certain late Byzantine interiors, especially of Russia and Greece. The proportions of the interior spaces here (low and massively constructed) are like those of the late medieval eastern Mediterranean rather than those of the contemporary late Baroque. The combination of a folk-artistic attitude in such details as the turned spindles of the doors and the irregularities of wall and painting strengthens a spiritual connection between the local interpretations of Byzantine grandeur and the local interpretations of post-Council of Trent Catholicism.

TLACOCHAHUAYA, GOD THE FATHER AS THE TRINITY, HOLDING A CRUCIFIX ON THE ORB, FLANKED BY SAN JUAN BAUTISTA AND SANTO DOMINGO (SCULPTURES) (pl. 74)

The almost doll-like hieratic majesty of God the Father is accentuated by the tipsy angles of the divisions of his tiara (signifying his impersonation of the Trinity). Again, it is the indefinable total quality of the *conjunto*, rather than the distinction of the sculpture, which makes these casual modern regroupings of older pieces memorable.

TLACOCHAHUAYA, CHRIST ENTERING JERUSALEM (SCULPTURE) (pl. 75)

Although the carving of man and beast are exceedingly rude in this piece of sculpture, and may well be more recent than 1800, the work points up an important aspect of much colonial Mexican sculpture —its compelling undercurrent of meaning, in even the least sophisticated and technically inept works. Indeed, some of the more folkloristic works are preferable to the jejune insipidity of a great deal of the later colonial painting and sculpture. Thus, though this work may have an actual date of 1750 or 1850 or even 1950, it is a timeless example of local identification with religious narrative at its most moving. The vacuous face of Christ might seem to some observers to be merely blank; yet it has a kind of compelling emptiness, anticipating the grave days ahead for Christ and their bitter dénouement. One can exaggerate these empathetic reactions, of course; the lank hair and the actual cloth robe would offend certain sculptural purists as does this identification with the sculptor's intent, if not his result. Still it is part of a touching naïveté, which can elsewhere set the Last Supper with cola bottles or place a wristwatch on the Infant Jesus. It is an inescapable part of the total effect of Mexican church interiors, especially today.

TLACOCHAHUAYA, CRUCIFIX ON A RETABLE (SCULPTURE) (pl. 76)

The emaciated, sinewy figure of Christ bends in a grimly realistic sagging curve. Curiously, however, the head has not yet fallen all the way forward; one senses a physical resistance, which this sculptor must have intuitively realized, paralleling the spiritual stiffening of the Crucifixion. Not so hideously flecked with blood as are most of the Mexican figures of Christ at the Column, there are savage touches here in the bloodied kneecaps and wounded legs which assert in a more discreet manner the tradition of torture from the pre-Conquest era. The retable upon which this figure is placed is again of about 1700, like the *retablo mayor*. It is difficult to know if the crucifix is exactly contemporary.

TLACOCHAHUAYA, ORGAN, *coro alto* (pl. 161, color)

The little organ cases of the eighteenth century in Mexico are among its most diverting works. A dated one at Santa Rosa in Querétaro (in the *coro bajo*) gives us one of the earliest examples of the approach of Rococo taste (1759). The organ case at Tlacochahuaya is also moving close to the taste for *rocaille*, but is not explicitly Rococo; like Ignacio Mariano de las Casas' work at Santa Rosa in Querétaro, it might be called Barococo—having still the richness of the Baroque and some of the lightness of the Rococo. Proof of its date would provide an exact correlative for the other painted decoration here, as the case has some of the same kind of painting as the vaults and walls. Aside from these scholarly problems, it is the frivolous character of the organ case that matters; it breathes the same fancy-dress playfulness as the angel in the vault. Its show pipes are encased in a *bouffant* confection of carved wood, which spirals giddily to a framed painting at the top. Below, the *chamades* (horizontal pipes) and actual keyboard suggest a practical side to this enchanting toy.

TLALMANALCO (México)

FRANCISCAN MONASTERY OF SAN LUIS OBISPO

A Franciscan *convento* at Tlalmanalco was finished by 1532–1533. The deeply respected Fray Martín de Valencia was buried beneath the *capilla mayor* of the church, and a special cult of veneration connected with the friar immediately developed. Kubler and Soria date the open chapel at Tlalmanalco to before 1567; Kubler connects it with the miracle-working body of the saint. In 1567 the body of Fray Martín disappeared from Tlalmanalco, and a new cult was established by the Dominicans around the Sacromonte at Amecameca, where Fray Martín had sometimes dwelt in meditation. Wilder Weismann prefers a date after 1584 for the open chapel, so that it might compete with the Amecameca shrine. A door of the church here is dated 1591 or 1691, which does not materially aid the dating of the open chapel.

TLALMANALCO, OPEN CHAPEL OF FRANCISCAN MONASTERY (pl. 17)

Kubler says this is "like a theater stage with a proscenium and diagonal side walls funnelling the attention of the crowd on the liturgy." Certainly it represents an attempt on the part of the friars to provide a sumptuous and dramatic setting for ceremony in the manner to which the Indians had been accustomed in the pre-Conquest era. Whether the structure was ever finished is difficult to say in its present ruined state. The ornamental enrichment of the arches is especially fine; in its lushness of motifs (an outstanding example of *tequitqui* carving, combining pre-Conquest motifs and vigor with European stereotyping), it could well be before 1567, although Toussaint and Wilder Weismann disagree on this stylistic dating, preferring a period in the 1580's. Certainly, its general character is closer to work of the 1550's at Huejotzingo than to known ornamental sculpture of the latter part of the century.

TLAXCALA (Tlaxcala)

FRANCISCAN CHURCH OF LA ASUNCIÓN DE NUESTRA SEÑORA

Founded in 1526, the Franciscan buildings at Tlaxcala underwent various campaigns of construction (one under Fray Martín de Valencia, who later went to Tlalmanalco). The present structures date from the later 1530's. Some rebuilding took place in the seventeenth century, possibly only in the form of adding various side chapels to the church. Interior additions continued into the eighteenth century.

TLAXCALA, MUDÉJAR CEILING OF FRANCISCAN CHURCH (pl. 23)

Among the finest *artesonado* ceilings in sixteenth-century Mexico is that of the Franciscan church at Tlaxcala. Following Islamic precedents which created similar wooden ceilings in Spain, these beamed roof systems had structural and ornamental parts wedded in a meticulous combination of carpentry and decorative geometry. The influential treatise on Mudéjar work, *Carpintería de lo Blanco* by López de Arenas, was not published until 1637. However, numerous sources were available for sixteenth-century workmen. Inlaid and gilded, this ceiling suggests the powerful impact that these intricately designed works had on all of later viceregal Mexico, especially in the wooden doors of churches and chapels.

TLAXCALA, CHAPEL RETABLES OF FRANCISCAN CHURCH (pl. 115)

Just as the Mudéjar ceiling of the Franciscan church at Tlaxcala is one of the best examples of its type in Mexico, so the retable here represents one of the high points of the Solomonic type. Of the same high quality as the retables in the Capilla de los Angeles of the Cathedral of Mexico, it must be dated to about 1700. There are still touches of a mannered ornament which persists from the mid-seventeenth century in Spain (especially in Granada), rather than anticipating the mannered ornament of the mid-eighteenth century in Mexico. Hollow twisted columns reveal a technical mastery which is also apparent in the dazzling foliate carving of all the background surfaces. By comparison the sculpture is disappointing, and indicates that considerable break between ornamental excellence and figural weakness which will run through more sophisticated works of the later viceregal era.

SANTA MARÍA TONANTZINTLA (Puebla)

SANTA MARÍA TONANTZINTLA

Lacking at the present time any definitive documentary evidence about the church of Santa María Tonantzintla, we can only say that it must date after 1690, and probably before 1730, although much of the interior decoration could well have continued farther into the eighteenth century (the *estípite* retables in the nave are probably *ca.* 1760). Tonantzintla has also been repaired in part more recently, or at least regilded and painted interiorly.

SANTA MARÍA TONANTZINTLA, GENERAL VIEW (pl. 108)

Although the name Tonantzintla technically refers to a great mother goddess of the pre-Conquest period, and its association with Mary, as here, is religious rather than geographical, one can only identify the group of churches with tiled exteriors and stucco interiors in this area by the last proper name of the full dedication of each tiny community, as San Francisco Acatepec or San Bernardino Tlaxcalancingo. Each church has an atrium, with the church dominating the space. Santa María Tonantzintla is the smallest and probably the earliest of the group. Its façade, facing like the others toward the two great volcanoes, Popocatepetl and Ixtaccíhuatl, is classicist Baroque in its simplest terms. The simple Tuscan pilasters seem to support a broken entablature; above is a small window with niches at either side and above. The top of the façade rises in a slight curve or semi-circular pedimental shape. More important than these details is the color—dull red tile with blue and white enrichments of glazed tile. The same color scheme is carried into the tile and stucco tower, which is a typical eighteenth-century staged form. Seen from the rear (the usual approach to the church through the town), the tower and dome attract one's attention immediately.

SANTA MARÍA TONANTZINTLA, CROSSING AREA (pl. 109)

Following the general Pueblan preference for elaborate stucco revetments of vault and wall surfaces (such as the Capilla del Rosario of Santo Domingo, finished in 1690), there is almost infinite variation of the foliation and cherub-filled inventions of the masters of Puebla itself. Aside from its Solomonic *retablo mayor* (in the lower center here), and other retables of the period between 1700 and 1760, the special character of Santa María Tonantzintla is dependent on the local bravura of its stuccoists. There is a pronounced folk character here, which has inevitably attracted the indigenists and elicited enthusiastic comparisons of this décor with "Indian" or "native" traditions. As suggested elsewhere in the text and catalogue of this book, there is comparatively little real "Indian" influence in Mexican viceregal art after 1570 or 1580. There is, however, a marked folk fantasy to much of colonial art, persisting down to the twentieth century. If the tinselly tones of parts of this particular interior reflect modern color harmonies rather than the suave harmonies of the eighteenth century (as in the undamaged *coro bajo* of San Francisco Acatepec or the *camarín* at the Santuario de Ocotlán), there is nevertheless an astounding vitality and exuberance manifest here.

TUXTEPEC (Puebla)

PARISH CHURCH (LA PARROQUIA)

TUXTEPEC, INTERIOR TOWARD RIGHT TRANSEPT, LA PARROQUIA (pl. 116)

The enthusiasm for all-over interior decoration of a church, apparent in the use of stucco or painting in many works of the eighteenth century, is less often seen in carved wooden paneling (as for example at Santo Domingo in San Cristóbal Las Casas). At Tuxtepec the walls are covered with magnificently Rococo paneling which is actually a kind of retable. Of course, the retables of the eighteenth century are a form of wall covering, as they virtually line the interior from floor to ceiling, as at Taxco. Unfortunately, the tendency to mix quaint or often tasteless nineteenth- and twentieth-century features (such as gaudy altar cloths, or cheap vases and paper flowers, or the most egregious examples of sentimental modern plaster saints and angels) with the more controlled taste of the viceregal era—which sometimes can produce an indefinably affecting *conjunto*—here sinks to artistic bathos. One can sympathize with the creative refurbishing of certain key monuments to obliterate partially these evidences of a gradually

declining middle-class taste; genuine folk taste rarely undergoes such degeneration. It is hard, then, in the twentieth century for many travelers to distinguish between these manifestations of past and present taste; and disputes about the need for "improving" certain interiors for these (as well as purely structural) reasons will continue to create problems.

TZINTZUNTZÁN (Michoacán)

FRANCISCAN MONASTERY OF SAN FRANCISCO

Though there was early work at Tzintzuntzán under Fray Juan de San Miguel, who accompanied Bishop Vasco de Quiroga to Michoacán, the present structures date principally from the last years of the sixteenth century, during rebuildings under the direction of Fray Pedro de Pila. An important façade and cloister are the remains of that era, as well as fragments of fresco painting and some sculpture.

TZINTZUNTZÁN, ENTOMBMENT OR PIETÁ (RELIEF), CLOISTER OF FRANCISCAN MONASTERY (pl. 163, color)

This comparatively unknown relief is one of the treasures of Tzintzuntzán. For many years in a forbidding, bat-filled room, it is a moving example of religious art, and can only be compared to a related Entombment in the Franz Mayer collection in Mexico City, of painted leather. It is quite possible that both are European in manufacture; certainly the one at Tzintzuntzán must have been executed by a master from the Peninsula. Suggestions of the work of Juan de Juni in the sixteenth century come to mind.

YANHUITLÁN (Oaxaca)

DOMINICAN MONASTERY OF SANTO DOMINGO

Founded in 1541, Yanhuitlán has a church that was probably begun about 1543 or as late as about 1550. The *encomendero* Gonzalo de las Casas was the principal benefactor, and it is said that he sent to Spain for the master architect and painter here. Apparently, however, the early work was improperly supervised, for the walls cracked. Work continued for about twenty-four years until the present massive church with its impressive flying-buttressed apse was finished.

YANHUITLÁN, GENERAL VIEW OF FAÇADE, DOMINICAN
CHURCH (pl. 46)

Related to the church façades of Oaxaca, not distant
to the south, the façade of Yanhuitlán's Dominican
monastic church must date from the later seventeenth century, although the curvetting cornice
which caps the whole central section would appear
more appropriate to the eighteenth century. Like
the Oaxacan façades, Yanhuitlán's is severely classicist with a regular pattern of Tuscan and Corinthian
half-columns (first and second levels) and Ionic pilasters (third level). The rather awkward relationship of the niches with their oversize, simple frames,
and especially the tentative feeling of the central relief in position against a plain wall, connect this work
with the façade of Santo Domingo in Oaxaca, which
is roughly contemporary in design and execution.
The Yanhuitlán frontispiece gains effect through its
isolated setting in "a wide and spacious valley"
(which is the translation of Yanhuitlán); its almost
monolithic appearance reminds one of the solidity of
Ávila cathedral in Spain, although Yanhuitlán is entirely divorced from the community once ranged
around it.

YANHUITLÁN, ENTRANCE GATE, FORECOURT OF DOMINI-
CAN CHURCH (pl. 47)

There are two stairs of access to the smallish forecourt
(it is hardly an atrium like those of, say, Huejotzingo
or Calpan) of the church. One leads up directly to
the façade and its court; the other (here) leads in
from the left side of the main frontal stair. A simple
arch, suggestive of a fragment of Maya building but
in fact entirely European, rises over ruined rubble
walls to lead the visitor again into the forecourt, from
a different point.

YANHUITLÁN, SIDE VIEW OF CHURCH WITH SIDE PORTAL
(pl. 48)

The side elevation reveals especially well the massive
masonry construction of this behemoth of earthquake-country monastic churches. The flying buttress
is, as Kubler has pointed out, simply a heavy stepped
pier buttress pierced with a small arch (again bring-
ing to mind a Mayan precedent in the construction
of the so-called Temple of the Magician at Uxmal,

Yucatan, where a small arched tunnel goes beneath
a massive series of actual steps). Two lofty pier buttresses frame the side portal, which, though related
to the Plateresque in certain bizarre columnar forms,
is essentially Renaissance with its coffered archivolts,
illusionistic half dome above, and general ornamental
language. The clerestory windows along the top of
the building are more definitely Gothic, especially
the one over the portal which has a traceried rose
window over its typical late medieval paired windows.

YANHUITLÁN, VIEW TO *retablo mayor* (pl. 49 and pl.
159, color)

This magnificent agglomerative interior reveals the
dynamic changes of fashion in viceregal Mexico. The
rib-vaulted nave, with its simple but effective patterns of main ribs, tiercerons, and liernes, the coffered domical apse (this semicircular apse is, of
course, rare in the sixteenth century), and the wall
tabernacles and fantastic filagree of strapwork above
—framing niches—on the triumphal arch are apparently all of the sixteenth century. The *retablo
mayor*, with its *salomónicas* and angled surfaces, like
the superb *retablo mayor* of Santo Domingo in Puebla, must be of the later seventeenth century and
was modified in 1718–1720. (Some writers, like Soria,
assign it to *ca.* 1575 and feel that the *salomónica*
columns are later replacements.) The paintings on
the *retablo mayor* are by Andrés de Concha. Along
the nave walls are a variety of smaller *retablos colaterales* from about 1700 to 1790, spanning most of
the fashion changes of the eighteenth century.

YANHUITLÁN, CHURCH DOOR TO CLOISTER (pl. 50)

This doorway poses a nice problem. The main elements of the carving are certainly sixteenth century,
and relate to the main door (and to a lesser extent
to the portal of the Porciúncula) at Xochimilco.
The stylistic affiliation here is as classicist as the
seventeenth-century façade of Yanhuitlán, but more
distinctly Herreran than simplified Baroque. However, the painting on the half-columns and on the
wall surfaces might well be later than the carving.
The suggestion of *salomónicas* in the foliated bands
on the half columns, and the lush character of the
rinceaux at the sides of the columns, point to a

seventeenth-century date—even as late as the early eighteenth century—and would relate this painting to that of Tlacochahuaya, which is of this later period. But this is only hypothetical.

YANHUITLÁN, MUDÉJAR CEILING UNDER CHOIR (pl. 51)

This extraordinary hexagonal-coffered ceiling in wood on the underside of the choir (that is, in the *coro bajo*) is one of the masterpieces of sixteenth-century craftsmanship. It must have been executed by a Spanish artisan, or very closely supervised by him. Each hexagon is a miniature domical shape, with a suggestion of the brackets or corbels and windows above that might be found in an Islamic dome. The rope patterns which rim the hexagons might be a late survival of the Manueline, or more simply a cord, as in the Franciscan cords used ornamentally in architecture. The pendent bosses are Renaissance with their floreate and leaf patterns and have a symbolic reference to the Dominican rose (rosary).

YANHUITLÁN, DETAIL OF A LATER EIGHTEENTH-CENTURY RETABLE, NAVE WALL (pl. 52)

The retable is conveniently dated to June 16, 1789. It is a late survival of the *estípite* type at this time, suggesting that Yanhuitlán was outside the fashionable areas of the eighteenth century (such as the then wealthy new mining towns of central and north-central Mexico). However, bunches of *rocaille* pattern are present to place it properly in the Mexican Rococo.

YANHUITLÁN, DESCENT FROM THE CROSS (RELIEF) (pl. 53)

Related in conception and period to the Pietá-Entombment from Tzintzuntzán, this Descent from the Cross of polychromed marble, generally dated to the seventeenth century, is above a side altar. The framing archivolts of the niche might be of the sixteenth century, although the marbelized paint and certain details suggest the era of 1800, as does the altar below.

YANHUITLÁN, SCOURGED CHRIST (SCULPTURE) (pl. 54)

Although both this and the image of death may have actually been made before or after 1810, they represent such important types of the colonial period that dates are unimportant. Their confrontation visually, although not actually at Yanhuitlán, emphasizes the underlying preoccupation with mortification of the flesh and physical degradation in Indian sacrificial practices and post-Conquest Christian images of sacrifice and death. It does not seem incongruous to the local parishioners to dress the image in the borrowed finery of their own time, simulating the mockery of Christ with pseudo-royal robes. What is most moving here is the obvious mestizo cast of the face, entirely removed from the European types of the earlier colonial period.

YANHUITLÁN, FIGURE OF DEATH (SCULPTURE) (pl. 55)

One of the most terrifying images of death in a country obsessed with death is this carved and painted wooden figure at Yanhuitlán. Forcibly recalling the numerous references to the skull in both pre-Conquest Indian and post-Conquest Catholic art, the work at Yanhuitlán could well have been executed early or late, and most probably was done about one hundred years ago or less. It is an archetypal representation of the Grim Reaper and brings to mind the equally primitive and awesome wooden sculpture of the Penitente cults of New Mexico in the United States.

YANHUITLÁN, CLOISTER (pl. 56)

Though not so grand as the great Augustinian cloisters with their high, elaborated ribbed vaults, this cloister was built in treacherous country and respects an earthquake potential here, as does the massive church. The low but well-proportioned Tuscan half-columns and the corbels which support the springing of the vault ribs are again in the severely classicist taste of the Dominicans, who tended to live more in monastic retreat than the Franciscans and Augustinians—and therefore perhaps placed more emphasis on these serene, simple cloisters.

YANHUITLÁN, CORNER OF CLOISTER (pl. 57)

Rimming the depressed arch here are Dominican roses in high relief; above, the wall entablature is a very simplified variant of the Doric or Tuscan, with an "incorrect" but effective dentil course under the cornice. The figures in the niche have been casually grouped, in a half-museum manner, more recently.

YANHUITLÁN, SANTO DOMINGO PROTECTING MEMBERS
OF THE ORDER (RELIEF) (pl. 58)

Provisionally located in a convenient opening, which
now serves as a niche, this carved wooden relief of
Santo Domingo protecting members of his order under an outstretched cloak has the semi-ruined surface condition which often is more appealing to modern taste than the impeccably preserved condition of
a few colonial works.

YURIRIA OR YURIRIAPUNDARO (Guanajuato)

AUGUSTINIAN MONASTERY OF SAN PABLO

Founded as a secular site, Yuriria was made an Augustinian settlement in 1550. Related in part to Acolman's Augustinian church, the group of buildings at
Yuriria is both more massive and more complex than
those at Acolman. The builder-director was Fray
Diego de Chávez, and work probably began in the
later 1550's and continued into the next decade, although some writers prefer a beginning date of 1540
and completion in the 1550's. Pedro del Toro is re-
puted to have been the *maestro mayor*. The building
was completed by Geronimo de la Magdalena. Buttresses were added to the church after 1625, and
there was interior work through the seventeenth century.

YURIRIA, FAÇADE, AUGUSTINIAN CHURCH (pl. 34)

The great church at Yuriria has a superb coffered
vault in the nave, unusual deep transepts, with crossing and apse covered in elaborate rib vaulting. Due
to constant menacing from Chichimec Indians (not
finally subdued until 1589), the fabric of Yuriria's
church and monastery is heavier and more fortress-
like than is usual in central Mexico. The façade,
closely related to Acolman's in its basic composition,
has a nervous network of strap patterns—turning into
foliation—investing all the wall surfaces, which are
left undecorated at Acolman. Fernández has called
this "tropical" Plateresque. The same combination of
Gothicisms and Renaissance ornament (including
the interesting plates of fruit on the underside of the
entrance arch, apparently based on similar ornaments in the principal sacristy of Sevilla Cathedral)
appear here as at Acolman, but the total effect is
somehow more local without becoming "Indian."

YURIRIA, CLOISTER (pl. 35)

One of the most important features of Yuriria's monastic complex is the magnificent cloister with tall
arched openings in the first level and stubby arched
openings in the second. At one corner an unusual
open staircase (not so large as the one at Actopan)
shows the primacy of the Hispanic world in the use
of major, open interior stairs of a squared, change-of-
angle type. The rib vaulting of the first level *portal*
or cloister arcade is as competent as anything of
contemporary Spain; and the half-columns framing
the arched openings and apparently supporting the
archivolts are relatively pure examples of the composite order—combining the best of Gothic in vaulting with the best of Renaissance in columns.

YURIRIA, CORNER OF CLOISTER (pl. 36)

Aside from the tranquil air of this cloister, it has a
number of interesting decorative features. Some, like
the fresco paintings, are closer to the construction
date of the buildings. Others, like these columns and
a fine bas-relief, are of various periods. The inscription below the columns says they came from a sixteenth-century retable in the parish church of Yuriria, burned in 1813. The columns and reliefs on
the right are of the sixteenth century, but the
salomónicas on the left are more likely of the late
seventeenth century and may have come from another retable or from a reworking of a sixteenth-century work.

YURIRIA, HOLY WATER BASIN, SECOND LEVEL OF CLOIS-
TER (pl. 37)

It would be almost impossible to date this simple
holy water basin or stoup and the relief of the Virgin
of Guadalupe over it. Representations of the Virgin
of Guadalupe were less common before the eighteenth century, when her cult was especially developed. This may be a rarer, early work or a primitive
example of the late viceregal period. It was the special strength of the local artist that he avoided the
sentimental qualities of so many later colonial images
of the Guadalupana; from technical "ineptness" he
made a more convincing work, aided by the ruin
of time.

ZACATECAS (Zacatecas)

CATHEDRAL (FORMERLY LA PARROQUIA)

Begun as a parish church in 1567, the Zacatecas structure was also worked on between 1602 and 1625 (under Francisco Jiménez). The building was reconstructed after 1718, and, though dedicated on August 15, 1752, was not finished until 1761. The interior was refurbished in 1852, and the parish church became a cathedral in 1864.

ZACATECAS, FAÇADE OF CATHEDRAL (pl. 132)

Dated by Toussaint to 1754, although probably executed over a fairly long time from, say, 1740 to 1755, the façade of the present Cathedral of Zacatecas is unique in Mexico. Carved from a brownish stone, it takes on new tonalities as the light changes. Legendary history likes to see in the fantastic proliferation of detail here the story of a condemned man prolonging his life by infinite variation. It is more accurately another extraordinary example of a deeply ingrained tendency in Mexico to cover all surfaces with a controlled pattern of ornament, which dates from pre-Conquest times and was reinforced by Plateresque and Baroque European trends. A similar type of all-over foliation, seen in certain parts of Peru, never quite attains the bravura of this particular work. It is unfair to call it provincial; it is neither a servile copy of the metropolis or an inferior conception (if one accepts its premises) to the best of European late Baroque. The composition is admittedly routine, slightly widening the traditional four-over-four articulation of one Mexican façade type. (There are, of course, two basic compositions—one squared and the other diminishing in width; Zacatecas combines them.) The rose window is anachronistic but well suited to this virtually Late Gothic riot of foliation. De la Maza in an article in *Mexico en el Arte*, No. 7 (1949), brilliantly described the iconography as well as the even more interesting schema of the side portals, which are as inventive as, or more inventive than, the main façade.

SAN AGUSTÍN

This church was converted to new uses in the nineteenth century; a side portal and cloister from the colonial building still suggest its quality.

ZACATECAS, SIDE PORTAL OF SAN AGUSTÍN (pl. 133)

This portal, once encumbered with new construction, has been once again exposed due to the enthusiasm of a group of local intellectuals. Only slightly damaged, it is related to works of the Guanajuato area, especially La Valenciana. Altogether conceptually more naïve than the side door of La Valenciana, here with a delightfully childlike relief, it nevertheless is ornamentally sophisticated and occupies a place in stylistic change between the *estípite*-framed main façade of La Valenciana and the purely ornamental side portal there. The niches here are framed with *estípites*, but they create ornamental niche-pilasters, which step forward in the brisk repetitions beloved at the end of the eighteenth century as one more way of animating a design.

PLATES

The arrangement of the plates is essentially chronological, to parallel the division of chapters ii and iii into the three great building centuries of the period between 1530 and 1810. Many buildings have important work of all three centuries—sixteenth, seventeenth, and eighteenth. In Mexico, therefore, it is particularly difficult to make an exact chronological arrangement of such dynamic subjects as architecture and art, affected by so many rethinkings, reworkings, and vagaries of local taste within the great changes of style.

In general, the era when the building had its most impressive architectural development is the deciding factor of its place in the main sequence. However, to give some sense of local relationships, all parts of a given complex (of whatever period) are grouped together. (The one exception—San Francisco at Tlaxcala—was necessitated by a problem in stylistic logic.) The arrangement not only provides a reasonable manner of studying the features of a complex ensemble but also indicates some of the dynamics of architectural and artistic change from era to era.

Special attention has been placed on visual interest in the organization of plates, implying sequence and providing contrast without too repetitious order of parts. At the beginning are the great monastic houses of the sixteenth century (Franciscan, Augustinian, and Dominican). Gradually the plates advance through the seventeenth century, the age of the maturity of the cathedrals, and then through the eighteenth, the age of glory for the parish and pilgrimage churches. Regional groupings and the geographic relationships that might prevail for a student or traveler are observed wherever possible.

1 HUEJOTZINGO, atrium and façade of Franciscan church

2   Huejotzingo, lower center of church façade

3   Huejotzingo, *portería* of monastery

4   Huejotzingo, northeast *posa*

5 Huejotzingo, detail of northeast *posa*

6 HUEJOTZINGO, nave vaults of church

7   HUEJOTZINGO, *retablo mayor* of church

8 CALPAN, façade of Franciscan church

9 CALPAN, south side of northeast *posa*

10 CALPAN, west side of northeast *posa*

11 CALPAN, northwest *posa*

12   CALPAN, east side of southwest *posa*

13   CALPAN, detail of east side of southwest *posa*

14   CALPAN, west side of southeast *posa*

15 CALPAN, detail of west side of southeast *posa*

16 TECAMACHALCO, general view of Franciscan church

17 TLALMANALCO, open chapel of Franciscan monastery

18 CUERNAVACA, general view of cathedral and open chapel
from north side of atrium

19 Cuernavaca, open chapel of cathedral

20 Cuernavaca, atrium cross of cathedral

21   Cuernavaca, side portal of cathedral

22 CUERNAVACA, staged tower of cathedral

23   TLAXCALA, Mudéjar ceiling of Franciscan church

24 ACTOPAN, façade of Augustinian church

25 ACTOPAN, church battlements

26 ACTOPAN, frescoed stair hall

27 ACTOPAN, refectory

28　ACOLMAN, façade of church

29   ACOLMAN, church interior toward *retablo mayor*

30 ACOLMAN, first cloister

31   ACOLMAN, second cloister

32 ACOLMAN, door in second level of second cloister

33 ACOLMAN, wall, Crucifixion (fresco), second
    level of second cloister

34 Yuriria, façade of Augustinian church

35   Yuriria, cloister

36 Yuriria, corner of cloister

37 Yuriria, holy water basin, second level of cloister

38 CUITZEO, general view of Augustinian church

39 CUITZEO, *espadaña*

40 Tepoztlán, façade of Dominican church

41 TEPOZTLÁN, *posa*

42 TEPOSCOLULA, open chapel of Dominican church

43   Teposcolula, detail, lower right center of façade
of Dominican church

44 Teposcolula, door to chapel of Santa Gertrudis

45 Teposcolula, interior of chapel of Santa Gertrudis

46 YANHUITLÁN, general view of façade of Dominican church

47 Yanhuitlán, entrance gate, forecourt of church

48   YANHUITLÁN, side view of church with side portal

49 Yanhuitlán, view to *retablo mayor*

50 Yanhuitlán, church door to cloister

51 YANHUITLÁN, Mudéjar ceiling under choir

52 YANHUITLÁN, detail of a later eighteenth-century
retable, nave wall

53   YANHUITLÁN, Descent from the Cross (relief)

54 Yanhuitlán, Scourged Christ (sculpture)

55 YANHUITLÁN, figure of Death (sculpture)

56 YANHUITLÁN, cloister

57 YANHUITLÁN, corner of cloister

58 Yanhuitlán, Santo Domingo Protecting Members of
the Order (relief)

59   Oaxaca, façade of Santo Domingo

60 OAXACA, stuccoed vault under choir of Santo Domingo: Tree of Jesse

61 OAXACA, vault section adjacent to Tree of Jesse under
choir of Santo Domingo

62   OAXACA, dome, Capilla del Rosario, Santo Domingo

63   OAXACA, San Mateo Evangelista from a pendentive of the dome,
     Capilla del Rosario, Santo Domingo

64   CUILAPAN, general view of two Dominican churches

65 CUILAPAN, interior of earlier church

66 CUILAPAN, choir area of second church

67   Tʟᴀᴄᴏᴄʜᴀʜᴜᴀʏᴀ, general view of Dominican church
and monastery

68 TLACOCHAHUAYA, atrium portal

69 TLACOCHAHUAYA, *posa*

70 TLACOCHAHUAYA, church interior toward *retablo mayor*

71 TLACOCHAHUAYA, pulpit

72 TLACOCHAHUAYA, church vault detail (fresco)

73 Tlacochahuaya, baptistry doorway

74 Tlacochahuaya, God the Father as the Trinity, holding
a crucifix on the orb, flanked by San Juan Bautista
and Santo Domingo (sculptures)

75 TLACOCHAHUAYA, Christ Entering Jerusalem (sculpture)

76   TLACOCHAHUAYA, crucifix on a retable (sculpture)

77 SAN CRISTÓBAL DE LAS CASAS, façade of Santo Domingo

78   SAN CRISTÓBAL LAS CASAS, side elevation of Santo Domingo

79   SAN CRISTÓBAL LAS CASAS, side portal of Santo Domingo

80   San Cristóbal Las Casas, chapel retable of Santo Domingo

81 SAN CRISTÓBAL LAS CASAS, detail of a
retable in Santo Domingo

82 SAN CRISTÓBAL LAS CASAS, pulpit of Santo Domingo

83   Oaxaca, façade of El Santuario de la Soledad

84 OAXACA, San Agustín (relief), façade of San Agustín

85 OAXACA, San Juan Evangelista (sculpture),
     façade of San Agustín

86 OAXACA, lower center of façade of cathedral

87 OAXACA, Assumption of Virgin (relief), façade of cathedral

88 OAXACA, detail of a panel beneath a figure niche,
first level, façade of cathedral

89 OAXACA, detail of pedestal, façade of cathedral

90 MÉXICO, D. F., relief from center of second level,
façade of Santo Domingo

91   México, D. F., San Agustín (sculpture), lower left
side of façade of Santo Domingo

92 MÉXICO, D. F., façade of San Juan de Díos

93 MÉXICO, D. F., façade of San Fernando

94   México, D. F., view of cathedral and El Sagrario from south side of Zócalo

95 MÉXICO, D. F., south façade of El Sagrario

96   Mᴇ́xɪᴄᴏ, D. F., interior of cathedral, crossing area

97 MÉXICO, D. F., north end of cathedral, with Altar (*retablo*) de los Reyes

98 MÉXICO, D. F., lower central section of façade,
    former Balvanera chapel of San Francisco (now Capilla
    de la Santa Escala)

99 TEPOTZOTLÁN, upper center of façade and tower of San Martín

100 TEPOTZOTLÁN, view to *camarín* and rear of façade
     of San Martín

101   CHOLULA, general view of pyramid and church of
      Nuestra Señora de los Remedios

102 PUEBLA, rear view of cathedral

103 PUEBLA, vault detail of Capilla del Rosario, Santo Domingo

104   SAN FRANCISCO ACATEPEC, church façade

105 SAN FRANCISCO ACATEPEC, San Francisco as Protector (relief)

106 SAN FRANCISCO ACATEPEC, Christ at the Column (sculpture)

107   SAN FRANCISCO ACATEPEC, The Dead Christ Mourned at
the Foot of the Cross (painting)

108   SANTA MARÍA TONANTZINTLA, general view

109   SANTA MARÍA TONANTZINTLA, crossing area

110   Tepalcingo, upper section, façade of El Santuario

111   Tepalcingo, detail, right lower side of façade of El Santuario

112 TEPALCINGO, Eve, from right side of door area,
    façade of El Santuario

113   OZUMBA, door of *la parroquia*

114   TEPEACA, side portal of El Tercer Orden

115 Tlaxcala, chapel retables of Francisan church

116   Tuxtepec, interior toward right transept of *la parroquia*

117   Taxco, general view of Santa Prisca

118   Taxco, relief, upper center, façade of Santa Prisca

119 Taxco, side portal of Santa Prisca

120　TAXCO, *retablo mayor* of Santa Prisca

121   PÁTZCUARO, view to San Agustín

122   MORELIA, general view of cathedral

123 MORELIA, façade of cathedral

124 MORELIA, tower of cathedral

125 Morelia, side portal of La Merced

126 MORELIA, general view of Las Rosas from
Plaza de las Rosas

127 MORELIA, upper levels of the paired façades
of Las Rosas

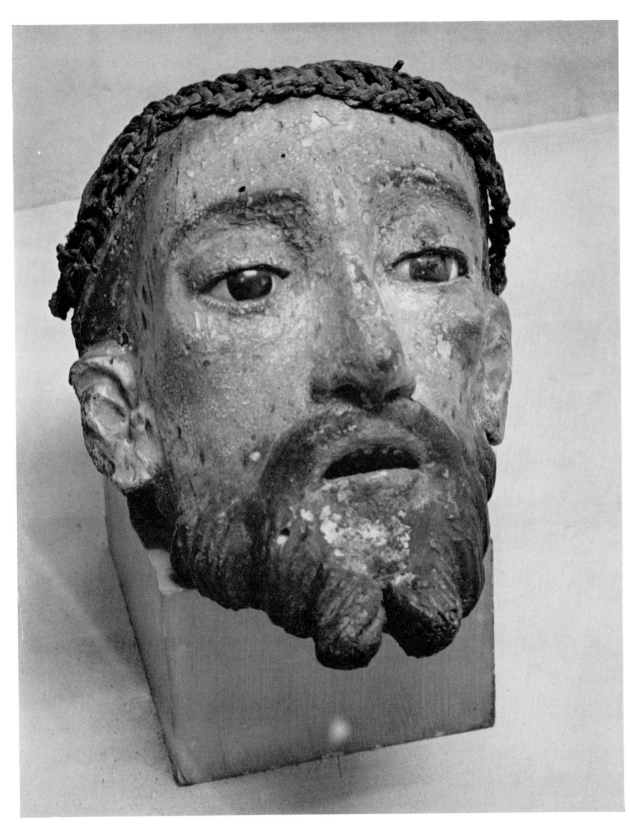

128   Morelia, head of Christ (sculpture) in museum

129 MORELIA, Sorrowing Madonna (sculpture) in museum

130   GUADALAJARA, one of the paired façades of Santa Monica

131 GUADALAJARA, San Cristóbal (sculpture)
at corner of Santa Monica

132 ᴢᴀᴄᴀᴛᴇᴄᴀs, façade of cathedral

133   ZACATECAS, side portal of San Agustín

134   SAN LUIS DE POTOSÍ, façade of cathedral

135 SAN LUIS POTOSÍ, upper center, façade of El Carmen

136   SAN LUIS POTOSÍ, lower center, façade of El Carmen

137 SAN LUIS POTOSÍ, wooden door, façade of El Carmen

138   SAN LUIS POTOSÍ, "proscenium" retable, left
transept of El Carmen

139   San Luis Potosí, entrance façade, Aranzazú chapel

140   Querétaro, side elevation of Santa Rosa de Viterbo

141 QUERÉTARO, cloister and unfinished tower of San Agustín

142 San Miguel de Allende, façade of El Oratorio

143 SAN MIGUEL ALLENDE, rear view of San Francisco

144 SAN MIGUEL ALLENDE, detail of façade of San Francisco

145　SAN MIGUEL ALLENDE, façade of El Tercer Orden

146   Lagos de Moreno, lower center of façade of *la parroquia*

147   GUANAJUATO, dome of San Felipe Neri from patio
      of the university

148   GUANAJUATO, façade of San Roque

149   LA CATA, façade of El Santuario

150 MARFIL, Crucifix (sculpture)

151 MARFIL, Madonna (sculpture)

152   La Valenciana, entrance stairs of San Cayetano

153 La Valenciana, detail of façade of San Cayetano

154   La Valenciana, side portal of San Cayetano

155 La Valenciana, general view of rear of San Cayetano

Color Plates

156   ACOLMAN, general view of Augustinian
      church and monastery

157   SAN CRISTÓBAL LAS CASAS, detail of façade
of Santo Domingo

158   SAN FRANCISCO ACATEPEC, detail of church façade

159   YANHUITLÁN, detail of *retablo mayor*

160   SAN FRANCISCO ACATEPEC, door to baptistry

161   Tlacochahuaya, organ, *coro alto*

162   Tepotzotlán, interior of *camarín*

163   Tzintzuntzán, Entombment or Pietà (relief), cloister
of Franciscan monastery

N

W   *E*

S